The Woman
Entrepreneur's Guide to
Success

UNLEASHING YOUR INNER POWER

Debra L. Caissie

Entrepreneurial Leadership Expert & Success Coach

Copyright © 2023 Debra L. Caissie
All Rights Reserved

To Chantelle,

Here's to you, my remarkable daughter. May your own journey be as inspiring to others as you've been to me.

Gratefully,
Mom

Introduction

Hello Beautiful Souls,
I'm Debra L. Caissie, and I'm absolutely thrilled to welcome you to a transformative journey, one that I've had the honor and pleasure to walk myself: the journey of "Unleashing Your Inner Power: The Woman Entrepreneur's Guide to Success."

You're here because you sense that deep, untapped reservoir of potential within you. You're here because you yearn for more: more fulfillment, more joy, more influence, and yes, more success. You're here because you're ready to shatter ceilings, break through barriers, and stake your claim in the world.

The empowering message in this book will provide you with actionable insights, practical tools, and invaluable wisdom collected from the front lines of entrepreneurial battles. We'll talk about everything from clarifying your desires to mastering the entrepreneurial mindset and finding your tribe—your community of supporters who will cheer you on as you take audacious leaps toward your goals.

And guess what? As you turn each page, you'll realize that your power was never something you had to earn or acquire. It's always been within you, just waiting to be acknowledged, nurtured, and released. I'm here to be your guide, your companion, and your biggest cheerleader as you embark on this life-changing voyage to unveil that immense power within you.

So, are you ready to make your mark? Are you prepared to embark on a journey that will not only transform your life but also positively influence everyone around you? Then buckle up; it's going to be an exhilarating ride!

Here's to the powerhouse that is YOU. I can't wait to see how you unleash your unique form of magic upon the world.

With love, light, and a whole lot of empowerment,
Debra L. Caissie

Contents

Introduction..4

Chapter One: The Journey Begins...........................10
   Uncover Your Life's Purpose..............................12
   Clarifying the Vision 16
   The Power of Self-Belief...................................18
   Lessons from Successful Women Entrepreneurs...................20
   Conclusion..23
   Questions...25
   Exercises..27
   Affirmation 30

Chapter Two: The Power of Desire..........................31
   Defining your 'Why'..35
   Turning your 'Why' into action 37
   Case Studies 39
   Conclusion..42
   Questions...44
   Exercises..46
   Affirmation 48

Chapter Three: The Action Imperative 50
   From vision to reality.......................................51
   Overcoming the fear of failure 56
   The role of discipline.......................................60
   So how do we develop discipline?......................62
   Thriving on challenges.....................................64

Conclusion 69

Questions 72

Exercises 74

Affirmation 76

Chapter Four: Unraveling the Resistance Wall 78

Recognizing resistance 79

Embracing change 82

Strategies to overcome resistance 87

Nurturing resilience 91

Conclusion 95

Questions 97

Exercises 99

Affirmation 101

Chapter Five: The Winning Entrepreneurial Mindset 102

Exploring the traits of successful entrepreneurs 104

Developing an attitude of learning, resilience, and adaptability 108

Embracing risk and failure 113

Power of positivity 117

Conclusion 121

Questions 124

Exercises 126

Affirmation 128

Chapter Six: Building the Balance Bridge - Work-Life Harmony 129

Work-Life Balance 130

Practical strategies for balance... 134

Real-life stories of women entrepreneurs 137

Mental wellness in entrepreneurship 139

Conclusion... 144

Questions.. 146

Exercises.. 148

Affirmation 151

Chapter Seven: Building Your Tribe 152

The power of networking 154

Finding your Mentors and Role Models 158

Empowering others... 161

The strength in community... 165

Leveraging diversity.. 169

Conclusion... 173

Questions.. 175

Exercises.. 177

Affirmation 179

Chapter 8: Stepping into Your Power.................................... 180

Celebrating milestones... 182

Reflecting on your journey.. 187

Planning for the future 191

Conclusion... 196

Questions.. 199

Exercises.. 201

Affirmation 203
Conclusion 204

"The future belongs to those who believe in the beauty of their dreams." - Eleanor Roosevelt

Chapter One:

The Journey Begins

Welcome to the first chapter of our shared journey, aptly named 'The Journey Begins'. I'm Debra L. Caissie and I am both excited and humbled to accompany you as we embark on a journey of personal discovery and professional growth. In this chapter, we will uncover the path that lies ahead and build the foundation for our entrepreneurial pursuits.

Every great journey begins with a purpose - a reason to venture into the unknown. Uncovering your life's purpose is not always a straightforward task; it requires deep introspection and the courage to face your true desires and talents. These are not small questions, but they are the compass that guides us in our entrepreneurial journey. Your unique gifts and how you wish to utilize them will form the bedrock of your entrepreneurial vision. Your purpose is not just about the destination, it's also about the journey. It's the lens through which you perceive challenges and opportunities, the motivation that keeps you going when the going gets tough.

Once we have clarity on our purpose, we can shape our vision. The vision for our entrepreneurial journey is much more than a business plan or a strategic blueprint. It's a holistic view of what we wish to accomplish, how we want to influence the world around us, and what we want our legacy to be. Our vision is like the North Star, a fixed point that guides us through the complexities and uncertainties of entrepreneurship.

But having a vision is not enough. You need to believe in it. This is where self-confidence comes in. Confidence is the fuel that propels us forward, the unwavering belief in our ability to turn our dreams into reality. We'll delve into the intricacies of self-confidence and discuss how to cultivate it, how to tap into it during times of doubt, and how to maintain it amidst challenges. It's important to remember that confidence is not about being fearless; it's about having faith in your abilities even when fear is present.

And to add to our understanding, we will glean wisdom from those who have journeyed before us. There's much to be learned from successful women entrepreneurs. These are women who started where you are now, faced the uncertainties, navigated the challenges, and emerged victorious. Their journeys, diverse as they may be, hold valuable lessons for us. They show us that success is possible, they inspire us with their resilience, and they teach us practical strategies to navigate our own journey.

The journey ahead won't always be easy. It will be filled with twists and turns, highs and lows, and a myriad of experiences that will both challenge and change you. But, like every great journey, it promises to be an adventure of a lifetime, an opportunity to grow, to learn, to inspire, and to make an impact.

So, let's take the first step. It's time to uncover your life's purpose, clarify your vision, ignite your self-confidence, and learn from those who have paved the way. This is where your journey begins, this is where you start Unleashing Your Inner Power. Remember, you're not alone on this journey, we're in this together, and I can't wait to see where it takes us.

Uncover Your Life's Purpose

As we commence this journey of unleashing our inner power, let's start by diving deep into understanding our life's purpose. A profound self-reflection is required to unlock this hidden treasure within us. It's a quest for authenticity and, in a way, a journey back to ourselves.

This leads me to wanting to share the journey of Maria with you. Visualize being underneath the vast azure skies, in the bustling heart of the city, where you'll find a small yet radiant flower shop named "Blossom's Delight". The shop was filled with vibrant tulips, serene lilies, passionate roses, and countless other species of flowers, filling the air with a melange of soothing fragrances. In the middle of this floral haven was its proud owner, Maria, a woman of unwavering determination and a heart full of dreams.

Every morning, Maria would wake up with the rising sun, eager to start her day. She would make her way to her cherished shop, opening its doors to the first golden rays of the morning sun. Each flower in the shop was a symbol of her dreams, her aspirations, her journey. She didn't simply see the shop as a business, but as an extension of her soul, an embodiment of her passion.

Maria was no stranger to the challenges of entrepreneurship. She had weathered her share of storms, facing them head-on with unwavering resilience. There were times when doubt crept in, when the trials seemed insurmountable, but Maria held steadfast. Her belief in herself was her guiding light, her anchor amid the tempest. It was this self-belief that had propelled her to transform her dream into a reality, to create a haven of beauty and tranquility in the heart of the bustling city.

Over time, Maria found herself being inspired by other successful women entrepreneurs. She found their journeys, their triumphs, and even their struggles resonating with her own. From their experiences, Maria learned invaluable lessons of resilience, passion, courage, perseverance, and authenticity. She incorporated these lessons into her journey, using them as steppingstones to forge her own path.

As the sun set each day, painting the sky with hues of orange and red, Maria would stand at the door of her shop, taking in the beauty of the day. It was a moment of reflection, a moment of gratitude. Each petal, each fragrance, each customer, was a part of her journey, a testament to her dreams, her passion, and her inner power.

And so, Maria continued her journey, day by day, step by step, blooming like the beautiful flowers that surrounded her. She was not just a florist, but a dreamer, a believer, an entrepreneur. She was a woman in bloom, rooted in her self-belief, nourished by her passion, and blossoming in her entrepreneurial journey.

I can affirm that the quest to discover my life's purpose was not a straight path. It was a winding journey that involved many moments of self-reflection and an openness to embrace my unique gifts. It's important to understand that everyone has a unique set of talents and abilities, which I like to refer to as gifts. These gifts are your superpowers; they set you apart from everyone else. But these gifts can only be beneficial when you recognize, appreciate, and find ways to utilize them in service to something larger than yourself. This is where your life's purpose comes into play.

Your life's purpose is the intersection where your passions, strengths, values, and impact on the world converge. It's the driving force behind what you do and who you are. It goes beyond the scope of your career or personal ambitions. It transcends the everyday routines and reaches into the realm of the meaningful and fulfilling.

Discovering this life's purpose often requires a deep dive into self-reflection. You need to ask yourself some hard questions and be open to the answers. What truly brings you joy? What are you naturally good at? What does the world need that you can provide? And most importantly, what would you still do even if you were not paid for it?

These questions may not have straightforward answers, but they guide you towards uncovering your life's purpose.

This journey of self-reflection is one that is deeply personal, and it's likely to evolve over time. You might uncover facets about yourself that surprise you. There may be talents that you've overlooked or passions that you've neglected over time. I remember a point in my own journey when I discovered a passion for empowering others, a gift for guiding those who are embarking on the entrepreneurial path. This passion was always within me, but it took a process of self-reflection and exploration to understand it and find ways to utilize it effectively.

It's important to remember that discovering your life's purpose is not a one-time event but rather a continual process of exploration and self-discovery. There may be times when you feel lost, but these moments are just opportunities to delve deeper, reevaluate, and readjust. The key is to remain patient, stay open to the journey, and keep exploring.

Uncovering your life's purpose is like setting a foundation for a building. It strengthens your entrepreneurial journey, provides clarity during uncertain times, and acts as a source of motivation when challenges arise. It's a compass that directs your actions and decisions towards meaningful and fulfilling goals.

Embrace the process of self-reflection and exploration, for it is in this process that we find our true selves. Discover and cherish your unique gifts and find ways to utilize them to impact the world around you. This is the essence of uncovering your life's purpose. And it's the first step towards unleashing your inner power as an entrepreneur. Remember, you are unique, your gifts are valuable, and your life's purpose is waiting to be discovered.

Clarifying the Vision

Once we've begun the process of uncovering our life's purpose and acknowledging our unique gifts, the next step on our journey is to clarify our vision. Vision is more than just a destination; it's a guiding principle that frames our entrepreneurial journey and serves as a roadmap for our actions.

When I began my entrepreneurial journey, clarifying my vision was a crucial step. A vision gave me direction, instilled me with a sense of purpose, and acted as a beacon of light in times of uncertainty.

Our vision should be a reflection of who we are and who we aspire to be. It should align with our life's purpose and our unique gifts. When we see entrepreneurship as an extension of personal growth, our vision becomes a blend of our professional goals and personal aspirations.

Entrepreneurship is much more than just starting a business, offering a service, or developing your brand. It is an opportunity to express our true selves, to create something that reflects our values and passions, and to have a meaningful impact on the world. Our entrepreneurial vision, therefore, should reflect these aspirations. It should resonate with our unique gifts, align with our life's purpose, and provide a sense of fulfillment and joy.

To clarify your vision, you need to envision what success looks like for you. And by success, I don't just mean financial gain or business growth. While these are important aspects, true success extends beyond these metrics. It could mean having a positive impact on your community, creating a healthy work-life balance, or achieving personal growth and self-fulfillment.

Your vision should inspire you. It should excite you and fuel your entrepreneurial journey. When you think about your vision, it should spark a passion within you, a desire to turn this vision into a reality.

Clarifying your vision is not always a straightforward process. It may require deep introspection and an honest assessment of your desires and values. It may evolve and change as you grow and learn. This is perfectly normal and a part of the entrepreneurial journey.

As we continue on this journey together, I encourage you to take the time to clarify your vision. Think about what you want to achieve, not just professionally, but personally as well. Reflect on your values, your passions, and your life's purpose. And most importantly, envision a future where you are living your entrepreneurial dream.

Remember, your vision is unique to you. It is a reflection of your journey, your growth, and your aspirations. It is an essential component of unleashing your inner power.

In the journey of entrepreneurship, having a clear vision is like having a roadmap. It may not predict every challenge or opportunity that comes your way, but it provides a direction, a sense of purpose, and a beacon of inspiration that will guide you in your journey. So let's embrace this process of clarification, for it will lead us towards a future where we are not just entrepreneurs, but fulfilled and empowered individuals making a difference in the world.

The Power of Self-Belief

In the realm of entrepreneurship, and life in general, self-belief holds a power like no other. It is the fuel that propels us forward, the force that urges us to take that leap of faith, and the resilience that enables us to persevere through the inevitable challenges.

As an entrepreneur myself, I can attest to the incredible influence of self-belief in the entrepreneurial journey. It's the unwavering faith that turns dreams into tangible realities. The very act of starting a business is a testament to one's self-belief. You are putting yourself out there, taking risks, and daring to believe that you have what it takes to succeed.

Self-belief is not about eliminating doubts or fears. On the contrary, it's about acknowledging them, yet choosing to believe in your abilities despite them. It's about looking at the mirror and seeing not just who you are but who you can become. It's about embracing the journey, with all its twists and turns, highs and lows, with the confidence that you are capable, worthy, and equipped to navigate it.

Self-belief starts from within. It's a process of acknowledging your unique gifts, appreciating your journey, and understanding your worth. It requires constant affirmation and self-love. It may not always be easy, and there may be times when your self-belief wavers, but it's in these moments that your true strength shines through.

Let's not forget that self-belief is also about humility. It's about knowing that it's okay not to know everything and it's okay to make mistakes. It's about understanding that every stumble, every roadblock is an opportunity for growth and learning. And it's about recognizing that your journey, unique as it may be, is a testament to your resilience and determination.

In the context of starting a business, self-belief is paramount. It empowers you to take action, to make decisions, to take risks. It allows you to envision success, not as a distant dream, but as a tangible goal within reach. It encourages you to push the boundaries, to innovate, to strive for excellence. And most importantly, it instills a sense of self-worth, a recognition that you are deserving of success.

Self-belief also extends to believing in your vision. It's about having faith in your ideas, your strategies, your potential for success. It's about standing strong in your convictions, even when faced with criticism or doubt. It's about believing in the value you bring to your customers, your industry, and the world at large.

In the chapters to come, we will delve deeper into the different aspects of entrepreneurship, each one intricately connected to self-belief. From ideation to execution, from facing challenges to celebrating victories, at every step of the way, your self-belief will be your guiding force.

So, as we continue on this journey of unleashing your inner power, I encourage you to tap into the power of self-belief. Embrace it, nurture it, let it guide you in your entrepreneurial journey. Believe in yourself, in your vision, in your ability to make a difference. Remember, you have within you a well of potential, a unique set of gifts, and a journey that is uniquely yours. And all it takes to tap into this potential is a leap of faith—a leap of self-belief.

Lessons from Successful Women Entrepreneurs

As we navigate the uncharted territory of entrepreneurship, there's immense value in learning from those who have already journeyed down this path. Specifically, the stories of successful women entrepreneurs offer a wealth of wisdom, inspiration, and practical insights. Their experiences, their triumphs, and even their struggles can serve as guideposts for us, providing valuable lessons and illuminating our path.

One recurring theme you'll find in the journeys of successful women entrepreneurs is resilience. They have encountered their fair share of challenges, roadblocks, and even failures. But what sets them apart is their ability to bounce back stronger, their unyielding spirit to push forward, and their remarkable strength in the face of adversity. From their experiences, we learn the importance of resilience in our entrepreneurial journey. We learn that setbacks are not the end of the road but rather steppingstones to our ultimate success.

Another key lesson from these trailblazers is the importance of passion. These women didn't just build businesses; they pursued their passions; they followed their hearts. They invested their time and energy into something they truly believed in. And it is this passion that kept them motivated, that fueled their drive, and that resonated with their customers. Their stories teach us that entrepreneurship is not just about earning a profit, but about creating something we love and believe in.

The courage of these successful women entrepreneurs is yet another lesson for us. They dared to break norms, to defy expectations, and to venture into unexplored territories. They took risks, made bold decisions, and stepped outside their comfort zones. Their courage reminds us to embrace the uncertainties of entrepreneurship, to take calculated risks, and to boldly step forward, even when the path is unclear.

From their journey, we also learn the power of perseverance. Success didn't come overnight for these women. It took time, patience, and relentless effort. They stayed the course, remained focused on their vision, and worked tirelessly towards their goals. Their stories teach us that perseverance is crucial in our journey, that success is a marathon, not a sprint.

Perhaps one of the most important lessons from these successful women entrepreneurs is the importance of authenticity. They stayed true to themselves, their values, and their vision. They built businesses that were a reflection of who they were, their passions, and their beliefs. They didn't compromise their authenticity for success. And it was this authenticity that set them apart, that connected them with their customers, and that drove their success.

As we move forward in our entrepreneurial journey, let's keep these lessons close to our hearts. Let's harness the wisdom of these successful women entrepreneurs, let's embody their resilience, passion, courage, perseverance, and authenticity in our own ventures. Let's learn from their journey and use these insights to fuel our own journey. Remember, every challenge is a lesson, every failure a steppingstone, and every success a testament to our inner power.

Conclusion

As we conclude this opening chapter of our shared journey, let's take a moment to reflect on the ground we've covered. It's been an exploration of inner landscapes and external realities. We've delved into self-reflection, identified our unique gifts, and learned how best to utilize them. We've framed our entrepreneurial journey as an extension of personal growth, understanding the need to constantly evolve and adapt in order to flourish.

We have also discovered the pivotal role of self-belief, acknowledging that the seed of every achievement begins with the belief in our capabilities. We've learned to recognize and embrace our self-worth, allowing this belief to propel us towards our entrepreneurial vision, even in the face of doubt or adversity.

Further, we've gleaned lessons from successful women entrepreneurs, absorbing their wisdom, courage, and resilience. These tales of triumph have imparted important lessons, taught us the value of authenticity, passion, and tenacity, and have shown us that setbacks can serve as steppingstones to greater heights.

As we draw this chapter to a close, let's affirm that this is merely the beginning of our journey. It's the foundation on which we'll build our dreams, step by step, brick by brick. A journey filled with exciting prospects, daunting challenges, exhilarating victories, and valuable lessons. But most importantly, it's a journey that promises transformation and growth, a journey that's uniquely ours.

As we move forward, remember that the journey of entrepreneurship is as much about the destination as it is about the voyage. It's about the person we become through our experiences, the lives we touch through our ventures, and the difference we make through our actions. It's about creating something that resonates with our values, something that reflects who we are and what we stand for.

As we forge ahead, let's not forget to celebrate our progress, no matter how small. Each step, each milestone, each achievement is a testament to our resilience, our determination, and our inner power. Let's take pride in our journey, in the path we tread, and in the footprints, we leave behind.

Remember, this is your journey. Embrace it, learn from it, grow through it. Harness your inner power, unlock your potential, and chart your own path. Believe in your vision, trust your journey, and always remember, the only journey is the one within.

As we embark on the subsequent chapters, let's carry forward the insights and wisdom gleaned from this chapter, applying them to our unique circumstances. With every page turned, let's continue to uncover, understand, and unleash our inner power.

So here we are, at the start line of our shared journey. Let's take a deep breath, a firm step forward, and with our vision in focus, let the journey begin.

Questions

As we embark on this journey of self-discovery and entrepreneurial spirit, I encourage you to open your mind and your heart to the questions that follow. The initial steps we take in Chapter 1: "The Journey Begins," are aimed at helping you uncover your life's purpose, identify your unique gifts, and start visualizing your entrepreneurial journey.

Each question has been carefully crafted to prompt introspection, stimulate your imagination, and spark your innermost desires. They are meant to take you deeper into your understanding of yourself, your goals, and your path forward.

These are not questions to be answered hastily. Instead, I invite you to take your time, to let each question simmer in your thoughts. The aim here is not just to find quick answers, but to cultivate a deeper awareness of your motivations, dreams, and potential.

Remember, this is your journey. There are no right or wrong answers, only your answers. They are steps along the path to unlocking your entrepreneurial spirit and shaping the future you desire. So, let's delve into these questions with courage, curiosity, and enthusiasm. Let your journey begin.

1. What unique gifts have you identified within yourself through self-reflection, and how can these be utilized in your entrepreneurial journey?

2. How does your vision for your entrepreneurial journey align with your personal growth and transformation?

3. How has the power of self-belief played a role in your past achievements, and how can it fuel your future entrepreneurial endeavors?

4. Can you recall a time when self-doubt hindered your progress? How did you overcome it and what did it teach you about the power of self-belief?

5. Who are the women entrepreneurs that inspire you, and what specific lessons have you gleaned from their journeys?

6. How have you incorporated resilience, passion, courage, perseverance, and authenticity into your journey so far?

7. As you conclude this chapter of your journey, how will the insights and wisdom gleaned be applied to the next stages of your entrepreneurial venture?

Exercises

Embarking on Chapter 1: "The Journey Begins," signifies the start of an exciting journey into the depths of your personal and entrepreneurial potential. To enhance this exploration and to facilitate deeper learning, we've carefully designed the following exercises. These are not just tasks to tick off a list but tools to harness your energy, awaken your entrepreneurial spirit, and pave the way for your growth.

These exercises are intended to move you from the realm of thought into the domain of action. They provide a practical framework to help you explore your unique gifts, clarify your vision, bolster your self-belief, and gain insights from successful women entrepreneurs.

Remember, the purpose of these exercises is not to attain perfection but to stimulate growth. There's no rush to complete them. Rather, take your time. Engage with each exercise fully and remember that the value lies as much in the process as it does in the outcome.

Each completed exercise brings you one step closer to your goals and dreams. They are the steppingstones on your path towards becoming a successful entrepreneur. So, embrace the journey, dive into these exercises with enthusiasm and openness, and let's begin this transformative experience together.

1. **Self-Reflection Exercise:** Set aside some quiet time for yourself where you can be undisturbed. Reflect on your strengths, talents, and passions. Write them down and think about how you can use these unique gifts in your entrepreneurial journey.

2. **Vision Board:** Create a vision board for your entrepreneurial journey. This could include pictures, phrases, or words that resonate with your personal growth and the goals you want to achieve. Keep it in a place where you can see it often to help maintain your focus and motivation.

3. **Belief Journal:** Start a belief journal where you write down positive affirmations about yourself and your capabilities. Examples could be "I am capable of achieving great things" or "I have the skills needed to be a successful entrepreneur." Revisit these affirmations regularly to reinforce your self-belief.

4. **Role Model Research:** Choose a successful woman entrepreneur who inspires you. Research about her journey, her successes, her failures, and what she learned from them. Identify the lessons that resonate most with you and think about how you can apply them to your journey.

5. **Resilience Reflection:** Recall a time when you faced a challenge or setback. Write about how you overcame it, the strategies you used, and how it made you stronger or more resilient. This exercise

can help you better understand your capacity to handle future challenges in your entrepreneurial journey.

6. **Authenticity Check:** Reflect on your values and what makes you authentic. Write down what authenticity means to you and how you can ensure your entrepreneurial journey aligns with your authentic self.

7. **Action Plan:** Based on the insights and lessons from this chapter, create an action plan for the next step in your entrepreneurial journey. Identify your goals, the steps you need to take to achieve them, and a timeline. This exercise can help provide structure and direction as you move forward.

Affirmation

Affirmations are like small seeds of positive energy that we plant into the soil of our minds. When nurtured regularly, they can blossom into beautiful realities that can transform the quality of our lives. As you begin reading "Chapter 1: The Journey Begins," I invite you to engage with the following affirmation. Let it guide your thoughts and actions as you embark on this exciting entrepreneurial journey.

Affirmation:

"I embrace the new beginnings that life offers me. With an open heart and a curious mind, I am ready to embark on this journey. Every step I take is a testament to my potential, my vision, and my unwavering commitment to succeed."

This affirmation is a gentle reminder that all great journeys begin with a single step—your step. Repeat this affirmation daily, especially when you're on the cusp of starting something new or venturing into the unknown. Allow the words to sink in, and let them fortify your resolve. Remember, the journey of a thousand miles begins with this affirmation: You are ready, you are capable, and you are enough.

> "Passion is energy. Feel the power that comes from focusing on what excites you." – Oprah Winfrey

Chapter Two:
The Power of Desire

Welcome to Chapter 2, my friends, "The Power of Desire." If Chapter 1 was about embarking on the journey, this chapter is all about what fuels that journey, that powerful driving force – Desire.

What is desire? Is it just a simple wish or an idle thought? No, my dear readers, it's so much more than that. Desire is the heartbeat of ambition, the pulse of dreams, and the engine that propels us towards our goals. Desire is the bridge between where we are and where we want to be, the compass that guides us on our journey towards success.

But desire, in its truest form, is not a fleeting passion or a momentary longing. It's a burning, relentless force that captivates our minds, fills our hearts, and guides our actions. It's the unwavering conviction that our goals are within our reach, the unshakeable belief in the fruition of our dreams. Desire is the voice within us that whispers, "Yes, I can," even when the world around us screams, "No, you can't."

In this chapter, we're going to explore the incredible power of desire and its role in our entrepreneurial journey. We'll delve deep into understanding why some desires have the strength to transform our lives while others simply fizzle out. We'll unravel the strategies to stoke the flames of desire and keep them burning, driving us forward, even in the face of adversity.

We'll also discuss how to align our desires with our actions, how to convert our burning desire into a plan of action that leads us closer to our goals. We'll explore the magical connection between desire and determination, between aspiration and action.

And perhaps most importantly, we'll learn how to harness the power of desire to transform not just our entrepreneurial journey, but our lives. We'll learn how to use our desires as a source of strength, a source of inspiration, and a source of unstoppable momentum.

So, here we are, ready to tap into the pulsating power of desire. Are you ready to kindle the fire within, to fuel your dreams, and to propel yourself forward? If your answer is a resounding "Yes," then let's dive into this invigorating journey of desire. Hold on tight, for we're about to set our hearts ablaze with the transformative power of desire. Let the journey begin!

Unleashing the passion

As we delve into the heart of Chapter 2, let's dive deeper into a concept that's synonymous with desire and absolutely essential for any entrepreneurial journey. Let's talk about passion.

Passion - it's a word we hear often, isn't it? But what does it really mean in the context of entrepreneurship? Is it just about loving what you do? Or is it something more? I believe passion, in the truest sense, is a profound love for your work, combined with an enduring resilience that keeps you going, even when times are tough. It's an intense emotion that stirs you from within and drives you towards your goal. It's the unwavering commitment to your vision, the insatiable curiosity to learn, the relentless pursuit of excellence.

In entrepreneurship, passion is not just a nice-to-have; it's a must-have. It's the secret ingredient that gives us the courage to dream big and the determination to make those dreams a reality. It's the spark that ignites innovation, the fuel that powers persistence, and the glue that holds everything together when everything else seems to be falling apart.

Unleashing your passion is about allowing this powerful force to guide you, to infuse your entrepreneurial journey with meaning and purpose. It's about letting your passion illuminate your path, brighten your darkest hours, and elevate your greatest victories.

But how do we unleash this passion? How do we awaken this potent force within us? Well, it begins with self-discovery. It's about exploring the depths of your heart, understanding what makes you come alive, what makes your heart race, your eyes sparkle, and your spirit soar. It's about finding that one thing you love so much that you would do it even if you weren't paid for it.

Next, it's about aligning your work with your passion. It's about shaping your entrepreneurial journey around what you truly love, allowing your passion to be the foundation of your venture. Remember, when your work becomes an extension of your passion, it ceases to be work; it becomes a joy, a delight, an adventure.

But unleashing your passion isn't a one-time act. It's a continual process, an ongoing journey. It's about continually nurturing your passion, stoking its flames, and allowing it to grow and evolve with you. It's about embracing challenges as opportunities for growth, setbacks as steppingstones, and success as the sweet fruit of your passionate endeavors.

As we progress in this chapter, I invite you to reflect on your passion. Ask yourself, what sets your soul on fire? What fills you with joy and satisfaction? What gives your life meaning and purpose? Let these questions guide you, inspire you, and help you unleash the passionate entrepreneur within you.

Remember, passion is more than just an emotion. It's a way of life. It's the heartbeat of your entrepreneurial journey, the rhythm of your entrepreneurial dance. So, let's dance to the rhythm of our passion, let's march to the beat of our dreams. Because when we move with passion, we move with power. And when we move with power, there's no limit to what we can achieve. So, let's unleash our passion and let it lead the way. The journey continues.

Defining your 'Why'

As we delve deeper into Chapter 2, let's take a moment to explore a crucial question that forms the bedrock of your entrepreneurial journey. That question is, "Why?" Why do you wish to embark on this journey? What is the deeper motivation that drives your entrepreneurial vision? What is your 'Why'?

Defining your 'Why' is one of the most critical steps in your entrepreneurial journey. It's like setting the compass for your journey; it keeps you grounded, focused, and motivated. It's that powerful source of motivation that stays constant, even as your goals evolve and your path meanders.

Your 'Why' is your guiding star. It helps you stay resilient in the face of adversity, gives you the strength to overcome obstacles, and provides you with the inspiration to keep moving forward. It's that deep-seated reason that fuels your passion, ignites your desire, and defines your purpose.

Your 'Why' is more profound than simply making money or achieving success. While those are important goals, your 'Why' digs deeper. It's tied to your values, your passions, your dreams, and your purpose. It's about who you want to become, what you want to achieve, and how you want to contribute to the world.

Defining your 'Why' isn't always easy. It requires self-reflection, introspection, and soul-searching. It requires you to peel back the layers of your aspirations, motivations, and desires, to find that deep-seated reason that stirs your soul.

When you find your 'Why,' it changes everything. It provides you with clarity, fuels your passion, and strengthens your resolve. It helps you make decisions that align with your purpose, take actions that resonate with your values, and create a vision that reflects your deepest desires.

Consider the story of an entrepreneur who wishes to build a network of sustainable schools. Her 'Why' isn't just about building a successful business; it's about making quality education accessible, promoting sustainability, and empowering the next generation to create a better world.

That's the power of your 'Why.' It's not just a reason; it's a calling. It's not just a goal; it's a mission. It's not just about achieving success; it's about making a difference.

As we continue our journey through this chapter, I encourage you to reflect on your 'Why.' Ask yourself, what motivates you? What inspires you? What stirs your soul and ignites your passion?

Embrace the journey of self-discovery. Embrace the quest to find your 'Why.' Because when you find your 'Why,' you don't just find a reason to start your entrepreneurial journey; you find a reason to continue, a reason to persevere, a reason to succeed.

Your 'Why' is your secret weapon, your greatest ally, your most potent source of motivation. So, let's discover it, let's define it, let's embrace it. Because when you have your 'Why,' you have everything you need to make your entrepreneurial vision a reality. So, ready to explore your 'Why'? Let's dive right in. The journey continues.

Turning your 'Why' into action

So here we are, continuing on our journey through Chapter 2, having delved into the power of passion and the importance of defining your 'Why.' But understanding your 'Why' is just half of the equation. The other half, the crucial bit, is turning this 'Why' into action. It's about converting your deep-seated motivations into tangible steps that bring you closer to your goals. It's about letting your 'Why' fuel your persistence, particularly when you're faced with challenges.

You see, the entrepreneurial journey is rarely a smooth ride. It's filled with highs and lows, victories and setbacks, progress and detours. There will be moments of doubt, instances of failure, periods of uncertainty. But this is where your 'Why' steps in. Your 'Why' becomes the lighthouse in the storm, guiding you towards your destination. It becomes the steadfast anchor, keeping you grounded amidst the chaos. It becomes the resilient force, propelling you forward when the going gets tough.

Turning your 'Why' into action is about making a commitment to your purpose, your vision, your dreams.

It's about taking that first step, even when the path ahead is uncertain. It's about waking up each day with renewed vigor and an unshakeable resolve to take one step closer to your goal.

And how does passion come into play? Well, your passion is the powerful catalyst that transforms your 'Why' into action. It's the fire that keeps burning, the energy that keeps flowing, and the drive that keeps you going. When your passion aligns with your 'Why,' you create an unstoppable force that can overcome any obstacle, surmount any challenge, and weather any storm.

Consider this scenario: You've discovered that your 'Why' is to create a healthier, more sustainable world. You're passionate about nutrition and environmental conservation. So, you decide to start a company that offers nutritious, sustainably sourced meals. Every challenge you face, every obstacle you overcome, brings you one step closer to fulfilling your 'Why.' Your passion for nutrition and sustainability fuels your persistence, driving you to keep going, no matter what.

Remember, every action you take, big or small, is a step forward in your journey. Every setback is a lesson learned. Every failure is a steppingstone to success. And every challenge overcome is a testament to the power of your 'Why' and the strength of your passion.

As we traverse further in this chapter, take a moment to reflect on your 'Why' and your passion. Think about how you can turn your 'Why' into actionable steps. Visualize your journey, envision your success, and let your 'Why' guide your actions.

Embrace your passion, fuel your persistence, and let your actions speak louder than your words. Because the true measure of your 'Why' isn't just in its depth, but in its power to inspire action, to fuel persistence, and to drive success. Ready to turn your 'Why' into action? Let's forge ahead. The journey continues.

Case Studies

As we journey deeper into Chapter 2, let's immerse ourselves in the stories of a few extraordinary women entrepreneurs. These are women who have harnessed their desire, defined their 'Why', and turned their passion into successful ventures. Their stories serve not just as an inspiration, but as a testament to the transformative power of desire in the realm of entrepreneurship.

One such inspiring story is of Sarah, who was always fascinated by the intricate beauty of handmade jewelry. From a young age, she had a deep appreciation for the time, effort, and skill it took to create each unique piece. This passion for artisanal craft was her 'Why.' After years of working in a corporate job, she decided it was time to pursue her true calling. She started her own online platform that promoted and sold handcrafted jewelry from artisans around the world. Today, her company is thriving, providing a livelihood for hundreds of artisans and bringing their beautiful creations to customers worldwide.

Then there is Sophia, a single mother who had a fervor for baking. She would often find solace and happiness in creating delicious, home-baked goods for her children. Her 'Why' was to share this joy with others. Despite many challenges, she transformed her small kitchen into a bakery business. Sophia's commitment to quality, her delightful creations, and her heartwarming story resonated with customers. Today, she owns a successful chain of bakeries across the city, bringing smiles to faces one sweet treat at a time.

Consider Maria, a woman passionate about eco-friendly living. From a young age, she was conscious of her impact on the environment and strived to minimize it. Her 'Why' was rooted in her commitment to sustainability. Recognizing the lack of stylish, sustainable options in the fashion industry, she started her own line of eco-friendly apparel. Through her perseverance and dedication, Maria has managed to make sustainability fashionable, leading a successful brand that's loved by conscious consumers.

Each of these stories tells a tale of desire transformed into action. Sarah, Sophia, and Maria harnessed their passion, defined their 'Why,' and turned their dreams into thriving businesses. Their journey wasn't always smooth, but their desire to succeed and their commitment to their 'Why' saw them through. They are shining examples of how passion fuels persistence and how desire can be transformed into a successful entrepreneurial journey.

As we conclude this part of Chapter 2, let these stories inspire you, encourage you, and embolden you. Reflect on your own 'Why' and how it can shape your entrepreneurial journey.

Every woman entrepreneur has a unique story, a unique 'Why', and a unique journey. What will be yours? It's time to write your own success story. It's time to let your desire guide your journey. Are you ready to harness your desire and transform it into a successful business? Let's continue the journey. After all, the most exciting chapters are yet to come.

Conclusion

As we round off Chapter 2: The Power of Desire, we find ourselves brimming with insights and inspiration. We have seen how powerful a tool desire can be in the entrepreneurial journey. It is that spark which ignites passion, the anchor that grounds us in our 'Why', and the engine that propels our actions.

Unleashing your passion, defining your 'Why', and transforming these powerful elements into tangible action, are vital steps in your entrepreneurial journey. We've looked inward, understanding how to harness our inner desires, and we've looked outward, learning from the journeys of successful women entrepreneurs.

Remember Sarah, Sophia, and Maria, whose stories we delved into? They didn't just teach us about the power of desire; they showed us how it's harnessed and transformed into action. They illustrated that our 'Why' isn't just a motivating factor, but a compass that guides us through the highs and lows of our journey.

We've realized that our desires, our passions, our 'Whys' aren't just dreams; they're a roadmap to our entrepreneurial future. Our passions aren't fleeting moments of enthusiasm; they're deep reservoirs of energy that fuel our resilience and determination. And our 'Whys' aren't just reasons; they are the very essence of our entrepreneurial spirit.

But simply understanding the power of desire is not enough. The real magic happens when we act on it, when we let it guide us, when we turn it into an energy source that fuels our entrepreneurial journey. Each step we take, each action we make, brings us one step closer to transforming our desire into a successful entrepreneurial venture.

Take a moment to acknowledge the journey you've embarked on. Embrace your desires, cherish your passions, honor your 'Why.' Let them guide you, inspire you, and fuel your actions. The journey ahead may be filled with challenges, but remember, it's your passion that fuels your persistence, it's your 'Why' that guides your actions, and it's your desire that defines your success.

As we close this chapter, I invite you to continue this exploration of self, this journey of entrepreneurship. The lessons we've gleaned from Chapter 2 aren't just theories and concepts. They're tools in your entrepreneurial toolkit, weapons in your arsenal, steppingstones on your path to success.

Are you ready to harness the power of desire? To turn your passion into a thriving venture? To transform your 'Why' into a successful entrepreneurial journey? Then let's continue our journey. Onward and upward, my fellow entrepreneurs, because our adventure is just beginning. The Power of Desire has lit the way, and I can't wait to see where our journey takes us next.

Questions

In Chapter 2: "The Power of Desire," we delved into the heart of your entrepreneurial journey, exploring the deep-seated desires that drive you towards your vision. The following questions are designed to help you reflect more deeply on this chapter's themes, encouraging you to understand your motivations, and to channel your passion into a powerful, driving force.

1. What are the deep-seated desires that underlie your entrepreneurial vision?

2. Why are these desires important to you, and how do they connect to your personal values and life experiences?

3. How does your 'why' shape your vision for your entrepreneurial journey?

4. How can your 'why' help you persevere through the challenges you might encounter?

5. What practical steps can you take to transform your 'why' into actionable strategies?

6. Can you recall any instances where your desire propelled you to overcome a significant hurdle or achieve a milestone in your life?

7. What are some of the inspiring stories from other women entrepreneurs that resonate with you, and why?

These questions are not just queries; they are prompts for self-exploration. As you answer each one, delve deeper, challenge your assumptions and try to see things from a new perspective. The more honest and thorough you are in your responses, the more profound and insightful your realizations will be.

Remember, this is your journey. Take your time to explore each question. There's no rush, no right or wrong answers, just an opportunity for growth and understanding. So let's embark on this journey of self-discovery, shall we? And watch as the power of your desire transforms your dreams into reality.

Exercises

In Chapter 2: "The Power of Desire," we embarked on an introspective journey, unearthing the passions and desires that form the foundation of your entrepreneurial vision. To further integrate the lessons from this chapter, I have created a series of exercises. These exercises are designed to deepen your understanding and help you harness your desires effectively.

1. **Desire Map:** Create a "Desire Map" detailing all the things you want to achieve as an entrepreneur. Be as specific as possible, writing down everything from the big goals to the small details.

2. **Visualize Your 'Why':** Spend at least 10 minutes each day visualizing your 'why.' Use all your senses to make this visualization as vivid as possible.

3. **Manifesto of Desire:** Write a personal manifesto that outlines your passion and desires. Make it as compelling as possible and place it somewhere you can see every day.

4. **Overcoming Obstacles:** Reflect on potential challenges that could arise in your journey and think about how your 'why' can help you overcome them.

5. **Transform Desire into Action:** Identify three actionable steps that you can take this week to bring you closer to your entrepreneurial goals.

6. **Role Models:** Identify three women entrepreneurs whose journey resonates with your desires. Study their approach, strategies, and how they used their 'why' to fuel their journey.

7. **Affirm Your Desire:** Craft a personal affirmation that encapsulates your desire and entrepreneurial vision. Repeat this affirmation daily.

These exercises are meant to not just make you think, but also to inspire action. Each exercise will require you to dive deep into your desires, visualize your goals, confront challenges, and explore real-world applications of your passions.

Remember, there's no right or wrong way to complete these exercises. They're personal and unique to your journey. The key here is consistency and authenticity. Be true to your desires and give yourself permission to dream big and aim high.

Embrace this process. Let these exercises stoke the fires of your desire and propel you towards your entrepreneurial vision. Your journey to entrepreneurial success starts from within, and these exercises are your compass. So, let's embark on this exciting journey together!

Affirmation

In this chapter, "The Power of Desire," we've learned how intrinsic desire, our 'why,' can be an immense source of energy and determination on our entrepreneurial journey. It fuels our vision, pushes us beyond our comfort zones, and propels us towards our goals.

One powerful way to constantly remind ourselves of our 'why' and maintain our momentum is through affirmations. Affirmations are short, positive statements that reinforce your goals and desires, enabling you to manifest them into reality. They help cultivate a positive mindset, improve self-belief, and keep your focus on your desired outcomes.

I invite you to embrace the practice of affirmations and allow it to guide you on your journey. To assist you in starting this practice, here is a specially designed affirmation for this chapter:

"I am a woman of fierce desire. My passions fuel my courage and determination. I am aligned with my purpose, and every step I take leads me closer to my entrepreneurial vision. I embrace challenges with open arms, for they are opportunities for growth. I am unstoppable."

Repeat this affirmation daily, ideally in the morning as you start your day, and whenever you need a boost of motivation or when doubt seeps in.

Visualize yourself living these words, embodying the truth they hold. Feel the passion, courage, and determination they stir within you. Let these words echo in your mind, guiding your thoughts and actions towards your entrepreneurial success.

Remember, the power of desire is immense, and when harnessed effectively, it can propel you to extraordinary heights. Embrace your desires, affirm them, and watch as you transform them into reality.

"The future depends on what you do today."
- Mahatma Gandhi

Chapter Three:
The Action Imperative

As we step into Chapter 3: The Action Imperative, I want to applaud you. We've traveled together through the journey of self-discovery, unraveled our deepest desires, and connected with our 'Why'. And now, my fellow travelers, we stand on the precipice of the next crucial phase of our entrepreneurial journey - action.

Here's a powerful truth: Ideas and dreams, no matter how grand, remain just that—ideas and dreams—without action. The most significant step between dreaming and achieving is action, the act of doing something rather than just thinking about it. This is where we move from contemplation to reality, from ideation to manifestation.

This chapter will be the launching pad for your journey into the world of entrepreneurial action. We'll dive into the nitty-gritty, the nuts and bolts of transforming your vision into a reality. It's time to roll up our sleeves and delve into the doing, because the heart of entrepreneurship beats in the rhythm of action.

The Action Imperative is all about understanding the importance of action, the nuances of goal setting, recognizing, and overcoming barriers, and maintaining that precious work-life balance while we're at it.

As we move forward, I urge you to embrace the spirit of action with an open heart and a determined mind. Allow yourself to feel the exhilaration of taking that first step, the thrill of seeing your vision take shape, and the satisfaction of progress.

Embarking on this phase of the journey may seem daunting, but remember, every great venture begins with a single step. So, let's lace up our shoes and step confidently into this new chapter of our entrepreneurial journey. Welcome to Chapter 3: The Action Imperative. Your future awaits, and it begins with action. Let's dive right in!

From vision to reality

Our first pit-stop is understanding how to turn our vision into reality. This is where the rubber meets the road, where your ideas transform from airy constructs into tangible, actionable steps.

This reminds me of a person I met named Zoe, a dynamic woman with dreams as high as the skyscrapers around where she lives. The entrepreneurial world beckoned her, whispered promises of innovation and fulfillment, yet something held her back. It wasn't the lack of a brilliant idea. She had one - an online platform for artisans to sell their unique, handmade products. It was fear. Fear of the unknown, fear of failure, fear of stepping into the vast expanse of entrepreneurship.

Every morning, she woke to the city's rhythm, a symphony of ambition and determination, her heart pulsating with the rhythm of her dreams. Yet, as the day wore on, her entrepreneurial spirit would fade into the background, drowned by her corporate responsibilities and obligations.

One cold winter morning, as frost clung to her apartment window, Zoe stood with her cup of coffee, gazing at the bustling city below. Something felt different. The city's rhythm was the same, but the melody she heard was different. It was a melody of action, a symphony urging her to step forward.

With a new resolution forming in her heart, Zoe sat at her laptop. Her hands hovered over the keyboard, uncertainty still lurking in the corners of her mind. But then, she remembered the symphony, the melody of action. She took a deep breath and began to type, crafting a business plan for her online platform. The fear was still there, but it no longer controlled her. Each word she typed, each idea she put into words, was an act of defiance against her fears.

Days turned into weeks. Zoe worked tirelessly, balancing her corporate job and her budding venture. She faced challenges and setbacks, but each time, she chose action over fear. Each challenge became an opportunity for growth, each setback a lesson learned.

The day finally came when Zoe launched her online platform. The city seemed to celebrate with her, the skyscrapers standing tall and proud, like silent cheerleaders. It was not just the launch of a platform; it was the victory of action over fear, of dreams over doubts.

Zoe's story is not about monumental success or miraculous transformations. It's a tale of everyday action, of embracing the power of doing over dreaming. It's a testament to the fact that when it comes to entrepreneurship, there's no force more powerful than the consistent, relentless, and determined action.

The key here is not to view action as a single, giant leap, but as a series of small, purposeful steps leading toward our grand vision. It's about breaking down our vision into manageable actions that make the journey feel less daunting and more achievable. As Lao Tzu, the ancient Chinese philosopher wisely said, "The journey of a thousand miles begins with one step."

Let's think about your vision as a giant puzzle. It might seem overwhelming to look at the complete picture on the box. But, if we start with one piece, then find another that fits, and another, we gradually begin to see the image take form. Each step you take is a puzzle piece, moving you closer to your full vision.

So, how do we begin translating our vision into actionable steps? It starts with clarity. Being clear about what your vision is, and more importantly, why it matters to you. We've touched on this in Chapter 2, defining our 'Why.' Your 'Why' is your compass, guiding your actions towards your vision.

Once you have your 'Why,' it's time to start setting SMART goals. Specific, Measurable, Achievable, Relevant, and Time-Bound. SMART goals act as steppingstones, leading you toward the realization of your vision. They provide a structure and trackability, making your vision less abstract and more attainable.

Overcoming the inertia of inaction can be challenging. It's akin to firing up a cold engine. But once you start taking action, momentum builds, and progress becomes visible. This breeds confidence, and confidence further fuels action. It becomes a positive, self-sustaining cycle.

And let me tell you, the magic truly starts happening when we take that first step. Our ideas cease to be confined to our thoughts and become something real, something that takes shape in the world. The ideas that once existed only in your mind's eye start taking form and influencing reality. Isn't that something to marvel at?

It's vital to acknowledge that action is not just about doing something for the sake of movement. Instead, it's about undertaking the right steps that align with your vision and ultimately guide you to your desired destination.

The concept of 'effective action' comes into play here. It's not enough to be busy; the question is, are we busy doing the right things? Remember, time is a limited resource, and it's imperative that we spend it wisely. It's important to discern between being 'busy' and being 'productive.' A hamster wheel keeps spinning, but it doesn't move forward.

But don't let this deter you. One of the incredible things about action is that it yields data, information. Every step you take, every decision you make, will give you valuable feedback. Whether it's a successful outcome or a setback, there's something to learn, something that can help refine your actions moving forward. It's a continuous process of 'act, assess, adjust, and act again.'

Building this feedback loop into your action process will allow you to make more informed decisions, refine your strategy, and better align your actions with your vision. Embrace this process. It's your roadmap to ensuring that every step you take is purposeful and leads you closer to your ultimate goal.

Yet, with all this talk about action, I want to remind you that it's equally important to pause occasionally. Pausing is not about inaction; it's about active rest. It's giving yourself the space to reflect on your journey, assess your progress, recalibrate if needed, and recharge for the journey ahead. Remember, entrepreneurship is not a sprint; it's a marathon. Consistent, sustainable action trumps frantic, sporadic bursts.

Action is the bridge between the intangible and the tangible, the dreamed and the realized. It's the magical process that brings our vision to life in the world around us. It's where the seeds of our dreams sprout, grow, and bear fruit.

Keep in mind, there will be setbacks and roadblocks. That's part of the journey. It's not about avoiding these obstacles but learning to navigate them. It's about dusting yourself off when you fall and resuming your journey with even more resolve.

Remember, it's not enough to have a great vision. It's not enough to have deep desire. We must also act. Vision, coupled with desire, fuels action, and action brings our vision into reality. So, as we venture forth, let's remember the importance of implementing our ideas into actionable steps. It's time to turn our vision into reality, one step at a time. Onwards!

Overcoming the fear of failure

As we delve deeper, we need to acknowledge an invisible force that can often hinder our journey to action - fear. Fear of failure, fear of the unknown, fear of rejection, or even the fear of success. All these fears and anxieties can become roadblocks on our path to entrepreneurship. They can paralyze us, keeping us stuck in the realm of 'what if' and robbing us of the potential for 'what could be.'

Let's first understand this: Fear is a natural human emotion. It's hardwired into our biology as a survival mechanism. However, when it comes to entrepreneurship, it's crucial to remember that fear is a compass showing us what we care about. It reveals to us what is important and thus, what we should face and conquer.

It's essential to recognize that fear and courage are two sides of the same coin. Courage is not the absence of fear but the decision that something else is more important than fear. This mindset shift can be a game-changer. Instead of viewing fear as an enemy, we can start to see it as a signal pointing us towards what we need to face to grow.

Now, let's explore some techniques to combat these anxieties and fears. One of the most powerful tools at our disposal is self-talk. What we tell ourselves can significantly impact how we perceive and respond to fear. We need to train our minds to focus on the positive, the possible, and the lessons to be learned. Instead of telling ourselves, "I'm afraid of failing," we can say, "I'm excited to learn and grow."

Next, let's consider visualization. Visualize your success, your journey, and the actions needed to get there. See yourself overcoming challenges, learning from failures, and celebrating victories. Visualization reinforces a positive mindset and helps subdue fear.

Also, remember the power of taking small steps. The larger the task, the larger the fear it can induce. Break down your tasks into manageable parts and celebrate each step as progress. As we've discussed earlier, even the smallest step towards your goal is a victory over fear.

Don't forget to leverage your support network. Share your fears and apprehensions with someone you trust, be it a friend, family member, or mentor. Sometimes, saying our fears out loud takes away their power, and getting a different perspective can help us see our fear in a new light.

Fear is a potent force, yet it's the response we choose that truly defines our entrepreneurial journey. It is the delicate dance between fear and action that ignites a transformation within us, enabling us to evolve into resilient and resourceful entrepreneurs.

As we continue to explore techniques to combat fear, let's delve into a powerful mindset that can serve as an ally - the growth mindset. Coined by psychologist Carol Dweck, this mindset is about embracing challenges, persisting in the face of setbacks, understanding that effort is the path to mastery, learning from criticism, and finding lessons and inspiration in the success of others.

To foster a growth mindset, start by accepting that you're on a journey of continuous learning. Each experience, especially those laced with challenges, is a chance to grow and enhance your skills. The entrepreneur's journey is riddled with uncertainty and surprises, but with a growth mindset, these become opportunities for innovation and improvement.

Embrace imperfection. Entrepreneurship is an art, not a science. Perfection is a mirage that often fuels fear. Instead of aiming for perfection, aim for progress. Every mistake you make, every failure you encounter is a steppingstone on the path to your success. Remember, it's not about how many times you fall, but how many times you get back up and keep going.

Practice self-compassion. Entrepreneurship can be a roller coaster ride, with highs of success and lows of failure.

When faced with setbacks, don't be hard on yourself. Understand that setbacks and failures are not reflections of your worth, but parts of your entrepreneurial journey. Extend the same kindness and understanding to yourself that you would to a friend in the same situation.

Adopt a 'what can I learn' attitude. When faced with fear or failure, ask yourself, 'what can I learn from this?' This simple question shifts your focus from the negative to the positive, from the problem to the solution. It turns every fear and failure into a teacher, guiding you towards better strategies and approaches.

Finally, recognize that fear will always be part of the journey. Fear doesn't mean you're not capable or that you're on the wrong path. It simply means you're human. It's a signal that you're stepping out of your comfort zone, challenging your limits, and daring to dream big.

As we move forward on our journey, let's wear our fears like badges of honor, a testament to our courage. With every fear we face, every challenge we conquer, we're not just becoming better entrepreneurs, we're becoming better versions of ourselves.

The path to entrepreneurship is indeed fraught with fear, but it's also laden with opportunity, growth, and triumph. As we continue to explore the Action Imperative, remember that fear is not a stop sign, but a steppingstone. It's an invitation to step up, take action, and embrace the incredible journey that lies ahead. So, let's march on, fearlessly!

The role of discipline

Our exploration brings us to an often-understated attribute, yet immensely vital in the realm of entrepreneurship - Discipline. Yes, this simple, unassuming word holds the power to transform our entrepreneurial journey and set us apart in the world of business. So, let's dive in and understand its significance.

You see, when we speak about entrepreneurship, we often hear about passion, creativity, and innovation, and while these are undoubtedly important, none of them can sustain the entrepreneurial journey without the backbone of discipline. Discipline is what keeps us on track when the excitement of a new idea wears off, or when we face obstacles. It is the steadfast force that holds our hand and guides us along the arduous path towards our goals.

Consider discipline as the bridge between your goals and your success. It transforms our dreams from mere thoughts into reality, turning our 'what if' into 'what is.' But, what does it mean to be disciplined? It is about consistency, resilience, and commitment. It is about doing what needs to be done, even when we don't feel like doing it.

Discipline begins with setting clear, specific goals and creating a plan of action to achieve them. It is about understanding what steps need to be taken and then, importantly, taking them. This might sound straightforward, but it is often where many aspiring entrepreneurs falter. We can have the most innovative idea, the most burning passion, but without the discipline to take consistent action, those ideas and passion will remain unrealized.

Discipline also involves managing our time effectively. As entrepreneurs, we often have multiple roles to juggle and tasks to handle. It's easy to get overwhelmed and lost in the maze of responsibilities. But discipline helps us prioritize and focus on what's truly important, enabling us to use our time and resources wisely.

Moreover, discipline is intrinsically tied to resilience. In our entrepreneurial journey, we are bound to face challenges and setbacks. But discipline empowers us to keep going. It builds a resilience that enables us to bounce back from failures and keep moving forward, one step at a time.

The beauty of discipline is that it's not an inherent trait but a skill that can be cultivated. It starts with small actions and decisions that, over time, become habits. It's about making the choice, every single day, to move closer to your goals.

In the realm of entrepreneurship, discipline distinguishes dreamers from doers, idea generators from innovators, and starters from finishers. It's the unsung hero behind every successful entrepreneur, quietly powering their journey from the realm of possibilities to the land of realities.

Moving forward, it's essential to remember that discipline is not merely about hard work, but it's about working smart. It's about focusing our efforts where they can create the most significant impact. It involves a clear understanding of our strengths, weaknesses, and resources, and using them to our advantage.

So how do we develop discipline?

Start by setting clear, attainable goals. What do you wish to achieve in your entrepreneurial journey? Define your vision and break it down into small, manageable tasks. These tasks should be steps that lead you closer to your larger goal. Remember, your goals should excite you and push you to stretch, but they should also be within reach so you're not setting yourself up for disappointment.

Next, create a routine that supports your goals. A structured daily routine provides a sense of order and predictability that can be incredibly grounding in the often-chaotic world of entrepreneurship. Be consistent with your routine. The true power of discipline shines through consistency. It's not about monumental actions, but the accumulation of small, regular actions that propel us forward.

Discipline also entails managing distractions. In our hyper-connected world, distractions are everywhere. From social media notifications to endless emails, these interruptions can easily derail our focus. Practice mindful attention, learn to prioritize, and set boundaries. Remember, every 'yes' to a distraction is a 'no' to your goal.

Moreover, develop the discipline of continuous learning. The entrepreneurial landscape is ever evolving, with new technologies, strategies, and trends emerging continuously. To stay relevant and competitive, you need to commit to learning and adapting. This doesn't mean you need to jump on every trend, but rather stay informed, and be discerning in adopting what aligns with your business.

And finally, embrace failure. Yes, you heard that right. Discipline isn't about avoiding failure. It's about learning to respond to failure constructively. Because let's face it, failure is a part of the entrepreneurial journey. But it's the disciplined entrepreneur who can take these failures, learn from them, and use them as steppingstones towards success.

As we reach the end of this part, let's pause and reflect. Discipline is more than a tool; it's a mindset, a way of life. It's about embracing responsibility, pursuing excellence, and committing to continuous growth. It's about taking control of our actions, our goals, and ultimately, our entrepreneurial journey. It requires patience, perseverance, and a whole lot of grit. But the rewards? Well, they're worth every ounce of effort.

As entrepreneurs, we're not just building businesses, but we're also building ourselves. And discipline is the cornerstone of this process. So, let's embrace it with open arms and open hearts. Because with discipline as our compass, we're not just charting our path to success, but we're also crafting a journey that's uniquely ours, marked with growth, resilience, and a whole lot of fulfillments. And isn't that what entrepreneurship is truly about?

Thriving on challenges

We arrive at an interesting crossroad – the intersection of challenges and growth. The entrepreneurial journey, as we know, is far from a smooth ride. It is riddled with twists and turns, obstacles and roadblocks. But what if I told you that these challenges are not just mere roadblocks, but rather, opportunities? Opportunities for growth, for innovation, and for strengthening your entrepreneurial spirit. That's exactly what we will explore in this section - how to thrive on challenges and use adversity to fuel your entrepreneurial journey.

Every entrepreneurial story is peppered with challenges. No one, no matter how successful they are now, has had a completely smooth path to success. Challenges are part and parcel of entrepreneurship. But, the crux of the matter lies not in the existence of challenges, but in how we approach them.

Consider challenges as hidden treasure chests. They appear as obstacles, but within them lie opportunities - opportunities for learning, for growth, and for innovation. They force us to step out of our comfort zone, to think creatively, to find solutions, and in the process, they stretch us, making us more resilient, more resourceful, and more adaptive.

Every challenge we overcome becomes a part of our entrepreneurial toolbox, arming us with new skills, insights, and experiences. They teach us invaluable lessons about our business, the market, and importantly, about ourselves - our strengths, our weaknesses, our limits, and our potential.

Moreover, challenges push us towards innovation. When we face obstacles, we're forced to think differently, to find new ways to do things. This is the breeding ground for innovation. It's in these moments of adversity that some of the best ideas are born, ideas that can transform our business and set us apart in the market.

But how do we shift our perspective from viewing challenges as burdens to seeing them as opportunities?

The first step is to cultivate a positive mindset. Adopting an attitude of resilience and optimism allows us to see the silver lining in every cloud and find the lesson in every setback. It's about viewing challenges not as stumbling blocks, but steppingstones towards our goal.

Next, practice problem-solving. Encountering challenges is inevitable, but how we approach them is in our hands. Develop a solution-oriented mindset. Instead of fixating on the problem, focus on potential solutions. Break down the challenge into smaller, manageable parts and tackle each one systematically.

Also, remember to stay flexible. Rigidity can be a hindrance in the face of challenges. The ability to adapt and adjust your plans based on the situation is a powerful tool in navigating obstacles.

I would love for you to picture your entrepreneurial journey as a beautiful mosaic piece. Each tile represents a different aspect of your journey. There are tiles for your victories, your joyous moments, your brilliant ideas, and your successful ventures. But there are also tiles for your challenges, your stumbles, your trials, and your doubts. It's this mix of tiles, this combination of highs and lows, victories and challenges, that creates the complete picture. And the beauty of it all is that each and every tile, no matter what it represents, contributes to the final masterpiece.

I understand that it's not easy to see the beauty of a challenge when you're in the middle of it. In those moments, challenges can seem overwhelming, daunting, even insurmountable. But remember that these moments are temporary. They are not indicative of your overall journey or your capabilities as an entrepreneur. In fact, these moments of adversity often serve as a launching pad, catapulting us into higher levels of growth, resilience, and success.

Embrace each challenge as a learning opportunity. Each one presents a chance to grow, to improve, to innovate, and to become a better version of yourself. And as you navigate these challenges, you'll discover that you're capable of far more than you ever imagined.

When we face challenges, it's easy to feel isolated, as if we're the only ones going through these hardships. But let me assure you, this couldn't be further from the truth. Every successful entrepreneur, every business leader you admire, has faced their share of obstacles. And it's their ability to navigate these challenges that has shaped them into the leaders they are today. They are proof that challenges are not only survivable but can also be transformative.

The road to success is paved with challenges. Each one is an opportunity to learn, to grow, and to become stronger. Embrace them, learn from them, and use them to fuel your journey. Because every challenge you overcome is another tile in your beautiful mosaic of entrepreneurship.

And always remember, the darkest night often heralds the brightest dawn. In the world of entrepreneurship, the depth of your struggles often determines the height of your success. The more challenges you overcome, the stronger you become and the higher you can soar.

So, the next time you encounter a challenge, don't despair. Instead, embrace it as an opportunity. It is your chance to grow, to innovate, to become a better entrepreneur. And who knows? It might be the very challenge that propels you towards your most significant breakthrough.

The journey of entrepreneurship isn't easy, but it is rewarding. Each step, each challenge, brings you one step closer to your dreams. And with every challenge you overcome, you become more resilient, more confident, and more prepared for the journey ahead.

So, take a deep breath. Brace yourself. Embrace the challenges and keep going. Because the journey of entrepreneurship is more than just a destination; it's about who you become along the way. Remember, you are stronger than you think, and your potential is limitless.

Keep moving, keep growing, and keep believing in your dreams, for it's only when you're tested that you truly discover who you are. And remember, the view is always better from the top!

Conclusion

As we draw to a close on this chapter, it's important to step back and reflect on the power of action. It's the unifying force behind every lesson, every insight, every piece of wisdom shared in these pages. It's not the mere act of thinking about our desires or planning our steps that brings about change - it's the act of stepping forward and taking decisive action that sets the wheels of transformation in motion.

Every idea, every desire, every vision you hold within your heart is potent with potential. And yet, potential alone is not enough. It is through action that potential becomes power; it is through action that dreams become reality. And so, as an entrepreneur, as a woman seeking to carve her path and make her mark, you must cultivate an intimate relationship with action.

At times, action might seem intimidating. After all, it's in action that we risk failure, face challenges, and encounter setbacks. But always remember, it's also in action that we discover our strengths, realize our capabilities, and ignite our growth. Each step you take, each move you make, is a testament to your courage, your tenacity, your resilience. Each action, no matter how small, brings you closer to your dreams and further from your fears.

Moreover, remember that action is more than mere movement. It's a statement. It's a declaration of your determination, your commitment, your resolve. It's a testament to your belief in yourself and your vision. It's the tangible manifestation of your inner strength, your resolve, and your passion. And every action you take is a building block, a stepping-stone, towards your dreams.

And yet, it's important to remember that the action imperative isn't about frantic hustle or relentless work. It's about intentional, purpose-driven action. It's about aligning your actions with your vision, your values, and your desires. It's about taking the necessary steps, one at a time, with a focus and determination that speaks volumes of your commitment to your entrepreneurial journey.

As we step into the subsequent chapters, we will delve deeper into the various facets of this entrepreneurial journey. We'll explore the landscapes of resilience, the terrain of balance, and the vistas of personal growth. Yet, at the core of it all, always remember the essence of action. For it's through action that we realize our potential, conquer our fears, and turn our dreams into reality.

And so, I encourage you, as you turn over to the next page, carry with you the lessons from this chapter. Honor the power of action. Embrace the journey of turning your dreams into reality. Harness the courage to step beyond your comfort zone and step into the vast, limitless expanse of your potential. Remember, you are the author of your destiny, the architect of your dreams. And with every action you take, you etch your story, you sculpt your journey, you paint your masterpiece.

The action imperative awaits you. The power to change, to grow, to succeed, lies within you. So step forward. Take action. And let your journey of transformation begin. Remember, you are not alone in this journey. You are surrounded by a sisterhood of women entrepreneurs who are walking this path, just like you. Together, we rise. Together, we conquer. And together, we transform our dreams into reality. Onwards and upwards, my dear. The best is yet to come!

Questions

As we delve deeper into Chapter 3: "The Action Imperative," we enter a pivotal phase of our entrepreneurial journey - the shift from planning to action. The questions that follow are intended to provoke introspection, foster self-understanding, and inspire decisive action.

1. What actions can you take today to move closer to your entrepreneurial vision?//
2. Can you recall a time when you overcame the fear of failure? How did you achieve it?
3. How do you plan to maintain discipline on your entrepreneurial journey?
4. Can you think of a challenge you recently faced? How did you overcome it, and what did you learn from the experience?
5. In what ways can you use adversity to fuel your growth and innovation?
6. What resources, tools, or people might you need to assist you in taking action?
7. How can you maintain momentum in your entrepreneurial journey, especially during challenging times?

The purpose of these questions is to guide you to an actionable mindset, one that embraces challenges, welcomes discipline, and celebrates every small step towards your vision. They are meant to be thought-provoking, encouraging you to look inward and forward.

Take your time answering these questions. Remember, the journey of entrepreneurship is not a sprint but a marathon. It's about consistency and resilience in the face of challenges. The insight you gain from these questions will help build a solid foundation for your future actions.

Let these questions be your guide as you take the imperative leap of action on your entrepreneurial journey. The path to your dreams begins with a single step. So, let's get started!

Exercises

As we forge ahead with Chapter 3: "The Action Imperative," we focus on transitioning from ideation to actualization. The exercises in this chapter are aimed at fostering a proactive mindset, preparing you for the inevitable challenges of entrepreneurship, and providing practical tools for action.

1. **Create an Action Plan**: Break your entrepreneurial vision into smaller, manageable steps. Identify the actions you can take immediately and those that will require more time or resources.

2. **Fear-Busting**: List the fears and anxieties you associate with starting your venture. Next to each fear, write a positive counterstatement or a possible solution.

3. **Develop a Discipline Routine**: Create a daily or weekly routine that promotes discipline. It might include time for planning, research, networking, self-care, and reflection.

4. **Adversity Brainstorm**: Think of a recent challenge and list the steps you took to overcome it. Identify the strategies that worked and how you can apply them to future challenges.

5. **Resource Identification**: List all the resources (human, financial, informational, etc.) that could support your entrepreneurial journey.

6. **Momentum Building**: Think of ways you can maintain momentum and enthusiasm, even when faced with challenges or slow progress.

7. **Vision Affirmation**: Write an affirmation that encapsulates your entrepreneurial vision. Use this as a mantra to stay motivated and focused.

Each of these exercises is a practical tool to apply the concepts of this chapter. They're designed to get you moving, help you build resilience, and ensure you're equipped for the journey ahead.

Remember, the key to meaningful change is consistent action. So, take your time, dive into these exercises, and watch as your ideas begin to take shape. They're not just tasks, but steppingstones on your entrepreneurial journey. Let's take that first step together, shall we?

Affirmation

In Chapter 3: "The Action Imperative," we focus on the importance of turning visions into reality. For this phase of your journey, I have prepared an affirmation that encapsulates the spirit of taking decisive, bold action.

Here is your affirmation:

"I am a doer, a mover, a visionary. With each step I take, I bring my dreams closer to reality. Fear is my teacher, not my enemy. I embrace challenges as opportunities for growth. I am disciplined, resilient, and unstoppable."

Affirmations are more than just words; they're potent reminders of our inherent power, our capacity to create change, and our resilience in the face of adversity. As you navigate through your entrepreneurial journey, this affirmation can be your mantra, a source of strength and motivation during challenging times.

Repeat this affirmation daily, preferably in the morning or at any moment when you need a boost of motivation or a reminder of your entrepreneurial spirit. As you say these words, visualize them in action. See yourself being a doer, a mover, embracing challenges and moving forward with resilience and determination.

Remember, affirmations are most powerful when they're personalized. Feel free to modify this affirmation to better suit your journey or resonates deeper with you. Let this affirmation inspire you, encourage you, and guide you as you take the imperative leap of action in your entrepreneurial journey. Let's harness the power of our words to fuel our actions!

> "It's not the absence of fear, it's overcoming it. Sometimes you've got to blast through and have faith." - Emma Watson

Chapter Four:
Unraveling the Resistance Wall

Have you ever felt an invisible force holding you back just as you're about to take a significant step forward? That's what we're going to delve into in this chapter.

You see, every journey towards growth and self-improvement, especially entrepreneurial ones, encounter this unique barrier known as the 'resistance wall.' It's an amalgamation of self-doubt, fear, uncertainty, and sometimes even past failures. It can sneak in subtly, planting seeds of apprehension, or it can be as blatant as a paralyzing fear of taking the next step. And it's more common than you'd think.

Understanding this resistance is an essential part of the journey. It's like a map to our insecurities and fears. By unraveling it, we gain a better understanding of ourselves, our dreams, our fears, and our true potential. But how do we begin this process? And more importantly, how do we use this understanding to our advantage?

In this chapter, we're going to dissect the resistance wall. We'll look at its components, why it emerges, and the impact it has on our entrepreneurial journey. We'll also explore ways to understand, navigate, and even leverage this resistance to our benefit. Remember, dear reader, each wall we encounter is not meant to stop us, but to help us discover how much we want something and how hard we're willing to work for it.

Embrace this chapter with an open heart and mind, ready to confront your resistance wall. The journey may be challenging, but the rewards - self-awareness, resilience, and unwavering determination - will be invaluable as you continue your path as a woman entrepreneur.

Recognizing resistance

In this exciting phase of our journey, we take a moment to pause and tune in to the subtler signals of our minds, the whispers of doubt and the echoes of fear that often hold us back. We are about to embark on the critical task of 'Recognizing Resistance,' the often-unseen barriers that can disrupt our path to growth and success.

Picture this scenario: You're fully equipped for your entrepreneurial journey. You have a solid plan, resources in place, and a passionate vision. Yet, something hinders you from moving forward. You feel a drag, a hesitancy that you can't put into words. This hesitation, dear reader, is the first sign of resistance.

Resistance is a tricky companion. It doesn't announce its arrival but subtly influences your actions, decisions, and even your beliefs. It makes its presence felt through the inner dialogue of self-doubt, the hesitation to embrace change, or the constant need to seek validation. It's a manifestation of our fears, doubts, and limiting beliefs.

When we talk about fears, they're not just about fearing failure or success. They can also be a fear of change, the unknown, or of stepping out of our comfort zones. These fears, no matter how trivial they might seem, can hinder our progress, making us second-guess ourselves, and in turn, impede our progress.

And then we have doubts. Doubts make us question our abilities and our worth. "Am I good enough? Do I have what it takes? What if I fail?" These doubts, when left unchecked, can evolve into limiting beliefs that define our capabilities and potential. They shape our reality and often sell us short of what we are genuinely capable of achieving.

Identifying these elements of resistance is not a weakness; in fact, it's an act of courage. It's about acknowledging that we are humans, susceptible to fear and doubts, but not defined by them. Recognizing resistance is the first step in asserting control over it, rather than allowing it to control us.

As we deepen our exploration of 'Recognizing Resistance,' let's remember that the resistance we face is an integral part of our journey. It is not the enemy to be vanquished; instead, it is a mirror that reflects our deeply embedded beliefs and fears, a tool to better understand ourselves.

It's natural for the concept of resistance to elicit unease. After all, it represents the parts of ourselves that we often prefer to keep hidden - the fears, the doubts, the limiting beliefs. However, I encourage you to approach this process with a spirit of openness and curiosity. As you begin to shine the light of awareness onto your resistance, you'll find that it loses its potency, and what seemed like insurmountable obstacles begin to feel more manageable.

Think of resistance as a language your mind uses to communicate its deepest concerns. It often emerges from a place of self-preservation, trying to keep us safe by avoiding risks and uncertainties. However, what was once a survival mechanism can become an impediment in our entrepreneurial journey, where risk-taking, stepping out of comfort zones, and facing the unknown are par for the course.

Remember the last time you tried to introduce a new habit or break an old one? Perhaps you decided to wake up an hour earlier to fit in some exercise or committed to limiting your time on social media. How long did it take before you found yourself hitting the snooze button or mindlessly scrolling through your phone again? That's resistance. It's that silent whisper, urging us to stick with what's comfortable, familiar, and safe.

In the entrepreneurial context, resistance can be even more nuanced. It might show up as procrastination, the incessant need for perfection, the constant seeking of validation, or even the inability to make critical decisions. Recognizing these patterns is the first step toward breaking free from them.

Resistance, however, is not the villain of our story. Instead, it's a sign that we are pushing our boundaries, moving out of our comfort zones, and venturing into the unknown. It is a sign of growth.

As we delve deeper into this chapter, we will explore various strategies to acknowledge and manage resistance. But for now, let's start with the recognition. Look within and see where resistance shows up in your life. Recognize its presence without judgment, understanding that it's merely a part of your journey towards becoming the best version of yourself.

And so, dear reader, I invite you to lean into this process of recognizing resistance with openness, curiosity, and kindness towards yourself. Remember, it's not about eradicating resistance but understanding it. For it's only through understanding that we can navigate its complexities and transform it into a catalyst for growth and personal evolution. This is your journey, and you have the power to shape it. So, let's continue, one step at a time, knowing that every step you take is a step towards your dream.

Embracing change

As we progress through this transformative journey, we now find ourselves on the precipice of an all-important concept: embracing change. The thread that ties us to our next monumental step is the acceptance that change is inevitable. It's a dynamic, fluid aspect of life, and the only constant we can truly rely on. The challenge, however, lies not in acknowledging this fact, but in genuinely welcoming it into our lives and finding our rhythm in its ebb and flow.

Understandably, change may stir up a whirlwind of emotions within us—excitement, anxiety, anticipation, fear. All these feelings are natural and valid. After all, change propels us out of our comfort zones, compelling us to face unfamiliar terrain and unexplored possibilities. But remember, while the prospect of change may seem daunting, it's also the driving force behind growth, innovation, and transformation.

Think about it. The decision to embark on this entrepreneurial journey itself was a significant change. You chose to step away from the familiar and venture into the unknown, driven by a burning desire to bring your vision to life. This choice was likely accompanied by a mix of trepidation and exhilaration. And yet, here you are, ready to embrace what comes next. That's the power of welcoming change.

Now, let's delve into some practical techniques to help us embrace uncertainty and manage change more effectively. One such technique is to cultivate a growth mindset. Instead of perceiving change as a threat, we can choose to view it as an opportunity for learning and growth. This perspective allows us to remain open and receptive, even when faced with unexpected turns.

When cultivating a growth mindset, it's essential to understand that this is a long-term process that involves reorienting our perceptions and attitudes. It's about shifting from a mindset of "I can't do this" to "I can't do this yet," viewing challenges as opportunities to learn and improve, rather than as obstacles. A helpful step in this direction can be to consciously remind ourselves of our past successes and growth moments. Recollect the times when you stepped out of your comfort zone, took on a challenge, and saw yourself grow and learn. These personal stories of triumph remind us that we are indeed capable of adapting and evolving.

As for mindfulness, a simple way to begin is to dedicate a few minutes each day to sit quietly, focusing on your breath. As thoughts and feelings emerge, observe them without judgment, let them come and go, like clouds passing by in the sky. This practice can help us become more aware of our emotional responses to change and uncertainty, allowing us to manage them more effectively. Additionally, mindfulness can be applied to our everyday activities as well—eating, walking, or even doing household chores. The aim is to be fully present, engaged, and intentional in each moment.

Now, let's turn our attention to resilience. One effective way to build resilience is through self-care. This encompasses physical care—proper nutrition, exercise, sleep—and emotional care—engaging in activities that bring joy, maintaining a supportive social network, and seeking help when needed. Remember, resilience is not about powering through difficulties at all costs. It's about understanding our limits, knowing when to push forward, and when to pause and take a step back. Another aspect of resilience is practicing self-compassion, which involves treating ourselves with the same kindness and understanding we would extend to a close friend. By being gentle with ourselves, especially during challenging times, we reinforce our emotional strength and resilience.

The journey towards embracing change is just that—a journey. It's a process of learning, evolving, and adapting, a continuous cycle of unlearning old patterns and cultivating new ones. And while this journey may be challenging, it's also an incredibly empowering and transformative one. So, let's take a deep breath, embrace the uncertainty, and open our hearts and minds to the endless possibilities that change brings. Remember, the winds of change, though unpredictable, can set us on the path to places we've never imagined, bringing us closer to our entrepreneurial vision.

This reminds me of a story I heard along my own entrepreneurial path. With a vision of creating a sustainable fashion brand, there was an inner flame burning in Tara. Yet, as she looked at the towering wall of resistance in front of her, she felt a twinge of fear. This wall, constructed with bricks of doubts, fears, and uncertainties, seemed like an insurmountable obstacle.

One day, while sipping her coffee and staring at her sketchbook filled with design ideas, Tara found herself pondering over her dreams. Each of her design sketches felt like a tiny light flickering in the vast darkness. The desire to bring these designs to life sparked a surge of courage within her. She realized that recognizing the wall wasn't enough. She needed to embrace it, understand it, and ultimately, dismantle it.

So, Tara started writing a letter, but not to a friend or a relative. She wrote to her resistance. She addressed her fears, each limiting belief, every flicker of doubt. "Dear Fear of Failure," she began, her pen gliding across the paper. As she wrote, she realized how much power she'd given to these fears and doubts. She was indeed more powerful than the resistance, not the other way around.

Change was inevitable, Tara knew. So, she started to work with it, not against it. She found solace in a quiet morning jog, where the rhythmic thud of her sneakers against the pavement gave her space to think, adapt, and plan for the day ahead.

Next, Tara reached out to friends who'd embarked on their entrepreneurial journeys. Their insights and experiences were invaluable. She learned about their struggles, their triumphs, and their resilience. She found a community, a network of support that assured her that she wasn't alone in her journey.

It wasn't an overnight process. Each step forward was met with a new challenge, a new fear. Yet, each setback didn't deter Tara; it made her stronger, more resilient.

One day, looking at the wall, she realized it wasn't as imposing as before. It was still there, but now, it didn't seem to tower over her. She had been unravelling it, one brick at a time, and in its place, she was building a bridge

— a bridge of resilience, courage, and perseverance, leading her towards her dream.

And so, Tara's journey continues. The resistance wall hasn't vanished completely, but now, she knows she's stronger than any wall that stands in her way. It was no longer about the wall of resistance, but about the power within her to overcome it. And with each passing day, she was turning her vision of a sustainable fashion brand into reality, one design at a time.

Strategies to overcome resistance.

As we travel through our entrepreneurial journey, understanding the resistance we face and learning to overcome it becomes a central part of our growth. It's like standing on one side of a dense forest, knowing that we need to cross to the other side. The forest may seem intimidating at first, filled with fears, doubts, and limiting beliefs. But once we equip ourselves with the right strategies, this forest transforms into a path towards self-discovery and growth.

One of the most potent strategies to combat resistance lies within our minds. Our mindset can either become our biggest obstacle or our strongest ally, depending on how we choose to perceive challenges. A positive mindset or what Carol Dweck describes as a "growth mindset," involves seeing challenges as opportunities for learning and growth, rather than as threats. It's about having faith in our capacity to evolve and adapt, cultivating a curiosity to learn, and viewing failures as information that guides us towards improvement.

Adopting a growth mindset doesn't mean ignoring our fears or difficulties. On the contrary, it involves acknowledging these feelings, yet choosing to focus on the possibilities and opportunities that lie ahead. When we encounter a challenging situation, instead of letting our inner critic take over, we can ask ourselves, "What can I learn from this?" or "How can I grow through this experience?" This shift in perspective doesn't happen overnight, but with conscious effort and patience, it can become an empowering tool in our arsenal.

Next, we have our support networks. These can be a source of emotional sustenance, practical advice, and a safe space to share our experiences and learn from others. Support networks aren't limited to friends and family. They can include mentors, peers, online communities, and even professional help, such as therapists or counselors. Building and maintaining these networks require effort and openness on our part. It's about seeking out connections, offering help, and being open to receiving it in return.

Now, let's talk about self-care. The entrepreneurial journey can often be demanding, physically and emotionally. It's easy to fall into the trap of relentless hustle, ignoring our well-being in the process. But sustainable success lies in balance, taking care of our mental, emotional, and physical health while pursuing our dreams. This could mean setting aside time each day for relaxation, practicing mindfulness, maintaining a healthy diet and regular exercise, or engaging in activities we enjoy.

Taking this journey further, it's important to note that while we're implementing these strategies, it's inevitable to face setbacks. Remember, setbacks are not roadblocks; they are merely detours that might require us to reassess our plans, gather more resources, or perhaps take a short pause to regain our strength. Just like a river finds its way around the rocks, we too can navigate around our challenges.

The beauty of the entrepreneurial journey is that it's uniquely ours. We set our pace, our rhythm, our style of overcoming resistance. We have the freedom to experiment with various strategies and stick to the ones that resonate most with us.

As we venture deeper into our journey, a powerful tool to tackle resistance is the practice of reflection. Regular reflection helps us to keep track of our progress, recognize patterns, celebrate victories and most importantly, learn from our experiences. Reflecting is not about dwelling in the past, but rather using our past as a learning resource for the future. We might journal our thoughts, meditate, or simply sit in silence, allowing our mind to sift through the events, emotions, and learnings of the day.

Reflection often leads to insights - about our selves, our journey, and the resistance we face. Insights that allow us to develop a deeper understanding of our resistance - why it arises, what triggers it, and how we typically respond.

This understanding empowers us to manage our resistance more effectively.

Let's also not forget the power of positivity and gratitude in this journey. Maintaining a positive outlook can shift our focus from the challenges we face to the opportunities that lie ahead. On the other hand, practicing gratitude keeps us grounded, reminding us of our accomplishments, our strengths, and the support we have in our lives. These practices nurture our inner strength, fueling our journey amidst the resistance.

Finally, it's essential to remember that overcoming resistance is not about achieving a state of zero resistance. Resistance is a natural part of our journey, a sign that we are pushing our boundaries, exploring unfamiliar territories, and challenging ourselves. Overcoming resistance is about learning to co-exist with it, managing it, and using it as a catalyst for our growth.

In conclusion, let's embrace the resistance we face in our entrepreneurial journey. Let's welcome it as a companion, a guide that directs us towards personal growth and self-discovery. As we adopt a growth mindset, build our support networks, practice self-care, reflect regularly, maintain positivity, and express gratitude, we transform this resistance into a powerful force driving us towards our vision. Remember, this journey is ours, and with every step, we are not just building a business but also crafting our masterpiece of resilience, courage, and growth.

Nurturing resilience

As we venture into the next phase of this enlightening entrepreneurial journey, we start to discover the true essence of resilience, often regarded as the entrepreneur's secret weapon. Resilience, at its core, is the ability to bounce back from setbacks and failures, to rise stronger and wiser, ready to face the challenges that lie ahead with renewed vigor and determination. This ability, this tenacity, doesn't just materialize out of thin air. It's something that's cultivated, nurtured and, over time, woven into the very fabric of our being.

Building resilience is akin to strengthening a muscle; it grows through consistent exercise and gradually becomes a part of our reflexes. So, how do we exercise resilience in our entrepreneurial journey? It all starts with acknowledging and accepting failure. This is often the hardest part. We live in a world that lauds success and often shies away from discussing failures. But, as entrepreneurs, we must break free from this mindset. Failures and setbacks are not the end of the road. They are simply steppingstones, lessons in disguise, preparing us for bigger challenges and greater successes.

Next, we need to adopt an attitude of learning from our setbacks. Each failure is packed with priceless lessons. It's up to us to unpack these lessons, learn from them, and use them to refine our approach. This requires a good deal of introspection and analysis, and it's here that the practice of reflection, which we discussed earlier, becomes vital. By consistently reflecting on our experiences, we can derive actionable insights that can inform our future course of action.

Now, it's not enough to simply learn from our failures; we must also apply these learnings. This application is the next crucial step in nurturing resilience. This could mean tweaking our business model, altering our marketing strategy, or even making some changes in our team. What matters is that we are making informed decisions, backed by our own experiences and learnings, thereby becoming better entrepreneurs with each passing day.

As we continue to build resilience, we must not overlook the role of self-care. While it may seem counterintuitive, taking care of our selves both physically and emotionally, is integral to cultivating resilience. Resilience isn't just about pushing forward at all costs; it's about knowing when to pause, recharge, and then resume the journey. A well-rested mind and body not only foster creativity and productivity but also prepare us to face challenges with a positive and determined mindset.

The beautiful thing about resilience is its universality. It's not exclusive to a chosen few. We all have the capacity for resilience, an innate strength that simply needs to be nurtured and harnessed.

Think about it this way - every single day presents us with challenges. We've all had days where everything that could go wrong, does. And yet, we don't just throw our hands up and surrender to the chaos. No, we grit our teeth, we take a deep breath, and we keep going. That is resilience in action.

In the entrepreneurial world, this inherent resilience is amplified. The journey of entrepreneurship is a rollercoaster ride, filled with exhilarating highs and daunting lows. The highs are celebrated, and rightly so, but it's the lows that test and shape us. It's during these challenging periods that our resilience is truly put to the test.

Building resilience, however, isn't a linear process. There will be days when we feel invincible, ready to take on the world. And then there will be days when everything feels overwhelming, when doubts and fears loom large. On these days, it's essential to remind ourselves that it's okay to feel this way. It's okay to have doubts. It's okay to feel scared. These feelings don't make us weak; they make us human. And acknowledging our humanity, with all its complexities, is a fundamental part of building resilience.

We also must remember that resilience isn't about masking our emotions or suppressing our feelings. Quite the contrary, it's about acknowledging our emotions and learning to manage them effectively. Emotions are a natural response to experiences, and they offer us valuable insights into our state of mind. So instead of pushing them aside, we should learn to understand and manage them. This emotional intelligence, as it's commonly known, is a crucial component of resilience and plays a significant role in our overall well-being and success.

As we cultivate resilience, we also cultivate optimism. An optimistic outlook empowers us to view setbacks not as insurmountable obstacles but as opportunities for growth. It enables us to focus on solutions rather than problems, thereby fostering innovation and creativity. Optimism, however, isn't about ignoring reality or blind positivity. It's about acknowledging the situation for what it is and then focusing on what can be done to improve it. It's this proactive and positive outlook that fuels resilience and drives progress.

In the end, building resilience is a journey, not a destination. It's a continuous process that evolves with us, reflecting our growth and learning. Each challenge we face, each setback we overcome, each success we achieve, adds another layer to our resilience, making us stronger and more adept at navigating the entrepreneurial journey. And as we continue to nurture and strengthen our resilience, we will find ourselves not just surviving, but truly thriving in our entrepreneurial journey.

Conclusion

What a powerful journey we've embarked on in this chapter. The Resistance Wall, as intimidating as it sounds, is not an insurmountable fortress but a series of hurdles, each one surmountable with the right mindset, tools, and strategies.

As we've explored in this chapter, the recognition of resistance is the first, crucial step. Like a splinter lodged deep, resistance often operates under the surface, influencing our thoughts and actions unconsciously. Yet, when we shine a light on it, acknowledging its presence and its influence on us, we start the process of dislodging it. By identifying our fears, doubts, and limiting beliefs, we take control of them, reducing their power over us.

Embracing change, a vital part of our journey, is often complicated by resistance. The unknown can be frightening, unsettling even. But let's remember that every significant journey begins with stepping into the unknown. We don't have to have it all figured out. We just need to take the first step, then another, and another. Techniques like mindfulness, visualisation, and journaling can support us in managing change effectively.

And what about those strategies to overcome resistance? We discussed mindset shifts, creating a supportive network, and employing self-care techniques, all critical tools in our arsenal to tackle resistance. We must remember that overcoming resistance isn't a one-time battle. It's an ongoing process, requiring consistent effort and commitment. But rest assured, each victory, no matter how small, takes us one step closer to our goal.

Perhaps one of the most critical aspects we explored is nurturing resilience, an indispensable quality for any entrepreneur. Remember, resilience isn't just about bouncing back from setbacks; it's about growing through them. It's about using adversity as a steppingstone, turning our trials into triumphs.

As we conclude this chapter, let's remember that resistance is not a sign of weakness or incapability. Instead, consider it a testament to our courage. For it takes bravery to acknowledge our fears and confront our limiting beliefs. It takes strength to stand in the face of change and uncertainty, ready to embrace them. It takes resilience to keep pushing forward, no matter the odds.

As we turn the page, let's carry these insights with us, using them as a compass to guide us. Here's to unravelling our resistance walls, one brick at a time, and building a resilient entrepreneurial spirit that thrives on challenges and grows through adversity. Onward and upward, my fellow entrepreneurs. Our journey continues.

Questions

Let's delve into some reflective questions that will help you better understand and manage your resistance. These questions are a chance for you to hold a mirror to your thoughts and beliefs. Don't shy away from any discomfort they may cause; that's where growth happens. So, take a deep breath and approach these questions with honesty and courage:

1. What forms of resistance have you identified within yourself when it comes to pursuing your entrepreneurial journey? Are they related to fear, doubt, or limiting beliefs?

2. Can you pinpoint any specific situations or triggers that heighten your resistance?

3. How do you typically respond to change? What are some ways you can become more adaptable in the face of change?

4. How have you tried to overcome resistance in the past? What worked, and what didn't?

5. Who are the people in your network that can provide support when you face resistance? How can they help you?

6. Recall a time when you faced a significant setback or failure. How did you respond, and what did you learn about your resilience?

7. Now that you understand your resistance better, what steps will you take to continue unravelling it?

Remember, these questions are not about 'right' or 'wrong' answers. They are tools for introspection and understanding. Take your time, be patient with yourself, and remember - growth is a journey, not a destination.

Exercises

Let's step forward with some exercises designed to help you unravel the resistance wall that might be standing between you and your entrepreneurial journey. Think of these exercises as actionable steps, small yet powerful tools that you can utilize to pave your way towards progress. There's no rush here; take your time and remember that every bit of progress counts.

1. **Resistance Reflection:** Write a journal entry about the forms of resistance you encounter most often. Detail the situations and feelings associated with them.

2. **Change Challenge:** Commit to one small change in your daily routine for a week. It could be as simple as trying a new breakfast item or waking up 15 minutes earlier. Journal your feelings and reactions to this change.

3. **Mindset Shift:** Identify a limiting belief that often triggers your resistance. Write it down, then write a counter-statement that reflects a positive, growth-oriented belief.

4. **Network Map:** Draw a simple map of your support network. Include people who inspire you, provide emotional support, or have skills and experiences that can help you on your journey. Beside each name, note how they can support you when you face resistance.

5. **Resilience Recall:** Write a story of a past failure or setback. Focus on how you bounced back from it, and the resilience skills you used.

6. **Self-Care Schedule:** Make a list of self-care activities you enjoy. Schedule at least one of these activities into your daily routine for the next week.

7. **Action Plan:** Now that you've identified your forms of resistance, write a detailed action plan on how you will overcome these. Break it down into small, manageable steps and set a timeline for each one.

These exercises might feel challenging at times, but remember they're designed to help you grow. Embrace the challenge and celebrate your progress. You're doing an amazing job!

Affirmation

Before introducing this affirmation, I want to assure you of the power it holds. Affirmations are a beautiful way of fostering a positive mindset, instilling confidence, and reinforcing the belief in our abilities. They may sound simple, yet their impact can be truly transformational.

Now, for our affirmation related to Chapter 4, Unraveling the Resistance Wall:

"I courageously acknowledge my fears, bravely embrace change, and steadfastly overcome resistance. With every setback, my resilience grows, leading me towards the manifestation of my entrepreneurial vision."

Say it out loud, feel each word resonate within you. Repeat it daily, especially when you feel resistance creeping in. You are powerful, you are resilient, and you can and will unravel any resistance that stands in your path.
You've got this!

"You gain strength, courage, and confidence by every experience in which you really stop to look fear in the face. You must do the thing you think you cannot do."
- Eleanor Roosevelt

Chapter Five:
The Winning Entrepreneurial Mindset.

Welcome to Chapter 5: The Winning Entrepreneurial Mindset. As we continue this journey together, it's time to delve into the heart of what makes a successful entrepreneur. That heart, my dear reader, is the mindset, the unseen force that guides our decisions, our reactions, and ultimately, our success.

I believe it's important to have a frank conversation about this, because having the right mindset can be the difference between a thriving entrepreneurial venture and a failed one. The entrepreneurial mindset isn't just about being ambitious, resilient, or even innovative, although those attributes are undoubtedly crucial. At its core, it's about embracing a holistic view of success, one that encompasses not just financial wealth, but also personal growth, happiness, and fulfilment.

This mindset is not about being immune to failure or rejection. Quite the contrary. It's about understanding that failure is not a dead-end but a detour, a signal that there's a different path meant for us. It's about turning setbacks into opportunities for learning, not barriers that hinder progress.

Furthermore, the entrepreneurial mindset goes beyond the scope of your business venture. It seeps into every aspect of your life, shaping your outlook, influencing your relationships, and determining your sense of self-worth. It's about realizing that you, as an individual, have the power to shape your destiny, your business, and your impact on the world.

But how does one cultivate such a mindset? Is it something we're born with, or can it be developed? And how does this mindset translate into tangible actions and decisions in our entrepreneurial journey?

In this chapter, we'll explore these questions and more. We'll delve into the key attributes of a winning entrepreneurial mindset, discuss strategies for developing these traits, and explore how to apply this mindset in various entrepreneurial scenarios. It's going to be an enriching journey, full of insights and revelations. Let's get started!

Remember, my dear reader, the journey to success is not a straight line. There will be ups and downs, twists, and turns. It's the mindset that helps us navigate these challenges and keep moving forward. It's our internal compass, guiding us towards our true north. It's the beacon of light that illuminates our path, even in the darkest of times. So, let's take this journey together and discover how you can cultivate your winning entrepreneurial mindset.

Exploring the traits of successful entrepreneurs

In our exploration of the entrepreneurial journey, let's take some time to consider the traits commonly found amongst successful entrepreneurs. It's important to note that there's no 'one-size-fits-all' approach to entrepreneurship, but there are indeed some characteristics that tend to be more prevalent in those who have effectively navigated the choppy waters of starting and growing a business. Now remember, my dear reader, these are not prerequisites to success, nor are they guarantees, but understanding them can offer valuable insight into the mindset that drives success.

Firstly, successful entrepreneurs often possess a high degree of self-belief. They have a strong confidence in their abilities and their vision, even when others doubt them. This self-belief isn't about arrogance or blind faith; it's grounded in their knowledge, their skills, and their unwavering commitment to their entrepreneurial venture. They know their worth, their potential, and they refuse to let others' skepticism dampen their spirit.

Another key trait is adaptability. Entrepreneurs who thrive understand that the business landscape is perpetually changing and evolving. They recognize the need to pivot, adapt, and evolve in response to these changes. It's not about abandoning their vision or their core values; it's about being flexible in their approach and strategies. They are comfortable with ambiguity, comfortable with not having all the answers, and they view this as an exciting part of the journey, not a daunting hurdle.

Resilience also plays a significant role in the entrepreneurial mindset. There's an adage that says entrepreneurs need to become comfortable with being uncomfortable, and there's a lot of truth in that. There will be setbacks, rejections, and failures along the way. It's the resilience to bounce back from these setbacks, to learn from the failures, and to keep pushing forward that sets successful entrepreneurs apart. They understand that every challenge is a lesson in disguise, an opportunity for growth, and they don't allow temporary obstacles to deter them from their path.

When examining the traits of successful entrepreneurs, it's crucial not to overlook the power of an inquisitive mind. Successful entrepreneurs are often naturally curious, constantly seeking out new knowledge, fresh perspectives, and innovative ways of doing things. This isn't just about staying up to date with the latest trends in their industry—though that's certainly important—but also about maintaining a broader curiosity about the world. It's this thirst for knowledge and new experiences that often fuels creativity and innovation, two key drivers of entrepreneurial success.

Then there is the entrepreneur's ability to envision a future others cannot see. This sort of visionary thinking, this ability to see beyond what is immediately apparent or presently possible, is at the heart of entrepreneurship. It's what drives them to create products that solve problems people didn't even realize they had, or to establish innovative services that change the way we live our lives. Having a vision isn't just about setting goals—it's about imagining the broader impact, the larger picture, and the potential to create something truly transformative.

Let's not forget the importance of persistence. Successful entrepreneurs are no strangers to long hours, hard work, and the constant juggling of responsibilities. They are persistent, determined, and unwavering in their efforts to build their businesses. Even when faced with failures or setbacks, they pick themselves up, dust themselves off, and get back to work. They understand that success is not achieved over night and that real, meaningful progress requires consistent and sustained effort.

And this brings us to another crucial trait: patience. Patience might seem at odds with the fast-paced, high-energy world of entrepreneurship. Still, it's an essential quality for any successful entrepreneur. Patience is about understanding that building a successful business takes time, that there will be detours and delays along the way, and that's okay. Patience is about recognizing that every step—no matter how small—is progress, and that the journey, with all its ups and downs, is just as important as the destination.

Let's discuss the impact of empathy. The best entrepreneurs often have a strong sense of empathy. They could understand and share the feelings of their customers, their team members, and others they interact with. This allows them to build strong relationships, create products and services that truly meet the needs of their customers, and foster a positive and inclusive company culture.

Finally, successful entrepreneurs have a deep sense of purpose. They are not merely driven by financial success or societal recognition. They are motivated by a bigger 'why,' a purpose that goes beyond the profit margins. They are passionate about their work, about the impact they are making, and this passion fuels their determination and their drive. Their entrepreneurial venture is not just a business; it's a calling, a mission, and this gives them the tenacity to overcome the inevitable challenges.

As we look deeper into these traits and how to cultivate them, it's crucial to remember that these are not static qualities. They can be nurtured, developed, and strengthened over time. The first step, however, is understanding these traits, recognizing their value, and being aware of their presence (or lack thereof) within us. Only then can we take the necessary steps to cultivate and nurture these traits within ourselves and fuel our entrepreneurial success.

I hope this exploration of the traits of successful entrepreneurs provides a starting point for you in your own journey. As we continue to explore these and other elements of the entrepreneurial mindset in the following sections, my hope is that you'll be inspired to delve deeper into your own mindset, to reflect, to learn, and to grow. Remember, the journey to success is not linear, and the road can be winding, but with the right mindset, any path can lead to your desired destination. So, let's continue this path together.

Developing an attitude of learning, resilience, and adaptability

I'm thrilled to delve into our next segment: the cultivation of a growth mindset. This concept, first coined by psychologist Carol Dweck, is a profound and powerful one. It essentially posits that our abilities and intelligence can be developed through dedication, hard work, and, most importantly, a love for learning. It's an attitude of resilience, adaptability, and continuous learning. When we adopt this mindset, we set ourselves up for lifelong learning and ceaseless evolution.

The importance of a growth mindset in entrepreneurship cannot be overstated. By its very nature, entrepreneurship is about charting unexplored territories and continually pushing boundaries. It requires the capacity to learn from every situation, adapt to changing circumstances, and bounce back from setbacks. And this is precisely where a growth mindset shines.

Imagine for a moment, the journey of entrepreneurship as a river. A river that's not stagnant but one that is continually flowing, ebbing, and changing its course as necessary. It's about being fluid, adaptable, and receptive to change. The ability to adjust our sails, to change course when needed, and to continue moving forward, no matter the obstacles, is central to the entrepreneurial journey. This ability is the epitome of a growth mindset.

Adopting a growth mindset also means recognizing that failure isn't a destination but an integral part of the journey. Each failure, each setback, isn't a signal to stop but a challenge to overcome, a lesson to learn. With a growth mindset, we see failures as temporary setbacks, not permanent roadblocks. They are opportunities for learning, for growth, for improvement. They are not ends but beginnings, not walls but doorways.

One of the most potent aspects of a growth mindset is the belief in limitless potential. When we embrace a growth mindset, we acknowledge that our abilities are not fixed or capped. We can always learn more, do more, be more. We understand that there's always room for improvement, always a higher level to reach. This is not about relentless pursuit or constant dissatisfaction, but about continual self-improvement and personal growth.

We must also remember that developing a growth mindset is not an overnight task. It takes time, patience, and continuous effort. It's about slowly but surely shifting our attitudes, adjusting our thought patterns, and altering our responses to challenges. But the beautiful part is that with each small shift, with each step towards a growth mindset, we're becoming better equipped for the entrepreneurial journey ahead.

As we continue this transformative journey, it's important to remember that a growth mindset is not just about embracing change or being open to learning. It's about wholeheartedly believing in the power of potential, our own and that of others. It's about fostering an environment of continuous evolution, where each experience, each interaction, and each challenge is viewed as a new opportunity for growth.

We often associate growth with external markers of success. However, with a growth mindset, growth is more about our internal journey. It's about self-improvement and self-awareness. It's about understanding that the most significant growth often comes from the most challenging experiences. That our most profound learning often happens in the face of adversity. And that our most meaningful progress often comes after our most significant setbacks.

Remember that time when you faced a problem that seemed impossible to solve? The one that kept you up at night, made your heart race, and your mind whirl with worry? But somehow, you managed. You persevered. You found a way to move forward. And in the process, you discovered strengths you didn't know you had, skills you didn't realize you possessed. That's the power of a growth mindset in action. It allows us to tap into our reservoirs of resilience, to discover our inner fortitude, and to harness our adaptability in the face of adversity.

Yet, the cultivation of a growth mindset goes beyond merely overcoming challenges. It extends to our everyday life and our interactions with others. It's about supporting those around us in their growth journeys, encouraging their efforts, and celebrating their progress, no matter how small. Because a growth mindset understands that every effort counts, that every step forward is a step towards growth, no matter how insignificant it may seem.

Cultivating a growth mindset also means celebrating our own progress. It's about acknowledging our efforts, appreciating our progress, and celebrating our small wins. It's about being gentle with ourselves when we falter, kind to ourselves when we fail, and patient with ourselves as we learn and grow. Because with a growth mindset, we understand that growth is not a linear process. It's a winding journey, filled with peaks and valleys, twists and turns, triumphs, and trials. And every step along this journey, no matter how challenging, is a step towards growth.

As we venture deeper into the exploration of a growth mindset, remember that this journey is a personal one. It's about your growth, your journey, your evolution. So be patient, be kind, and most importantly, be open to growth.

This leads me to a story of a wonderful woman I met at a trade show and how she beautifully pushed through her fears with a positive mindset. Here is her story.

Mia was as vibrant and dynamic as the city she called home. Having recently graduated from university, Mia found herself standing at the precipice of an exciting but uncertain journey: entrepreneurship.

Her dream? To breathe life into her unique concept of a sustainable fashion brand. A brand that not only showcased creativity and style but also upheld environmental responsibility. Yet, as she stood on the edge of this entrepreneurial expedition, fear and doubt cast long shadows over her enthusiasm.

"Am I capable enough?" "Can I really pull this off?" "What if I fail?" Questions like these were frequent visitors in Mia's mind.

But then, Mia remembered something her grandmother used to say, "Our minds are like gardens, dear. If we feed it doubt, it grows weeds. But if we feed it belief and positivity, it grows flowers." The words resonated with Mia.

In that moment, she made a conscious choice. She chose to harness her fears and doubts, to transform them into fuel for her entrepreneurial journey. The idea of failure no longer daunted her; instead, it became a part of her learning process, a steppingstone toward success.

With a renewed sense of purpose, Mia set to work. Each day, she encountered new challenges, but she met each one with determination and resilience. She nurtured a growth mindset, embracing each setback as an opportunity for learning and improvement. She was committed to her dream and refused to be swayed by temporary obstacles.

There were days when negativity and criticism threatened to diminish her optimism. But Mia, armed with her powerful positivity, pushed back against the tides of pessimism. She believed in her vision, in her ability to make a difference. She was not merely hopeful about her venture; she was confident. This confidence emanated from her unwavering belief in herself and her mission.

As months rolled into years, Mia's sustainable fashion brand bloomed. It wasn't an overnight success, and it wasn't without its fair share of challenges. But Mia's winning entrepreneurial mindset, her resilience, positivity, and growth-oriented attitude, navigated her through every hurdle.

And so, amidst the city of dreams, Mia, too, built her dream. Her journey was a testament to the power of a winning entrepreneurial mindset. A testament to the idea that the right mindset isn't just about succeeding in business; it's about overcoming doubts, embracing challenges, and persisting against all odds. It's about believing in oneself and one's ability to create change, just as Mia had believed in herself and her vision for a sustainable fashion future.

Embracing risk and failure

Risk and failure. Two words that evoke feelings of fear and discomfort in many of us. And yet, as we move further along our entrepreneurial journey, we find these two elements play a pivotal role. They become integral aspects of our path, not only as entrepreneurs but as individuals seeking to learn, evolve, and grow.

We've all heard the saying, "No risk, no reward." While this adage might sound like a cliche, it's an essential component of the entrepreneurial mindset. Taking risks involves stepping out of our comfort zone, challenging our boundaries, and venturing into the unknown. It's about not letting the fear of uncertainty hold us back. Instead, it's choosing to move forward with the understanding that while we can't always predict the outcome, we can always control our approach, our attitude, and our actions.

Embracing risk doesn't mean throwing caution to the wind. It doesn't mean making hasty decisions without due diligence. It's about making informed choices, grounded in research, analysis, and intuition. It's about trusting ourselves, our vision, and our ability to navigate the journey, even when the path isn't clearly marked.

And what about failure? For many of us, the fear of failure is what holds us back. We fear making mistakes, we fear being judged, we fear not living up to expectations - our own and those of others. But within the entrepreneurial mindset, we see failure differently. It's not a dead end. It's not a label. It's not a definition of who we are or what we're capable of achieving.

Instead, we reframe failure as an opportunity to learn. It becomes a teacher, offering invaluable lessons that books, lectures, or success itself cannot provide. When we stumble, we gain insights into what doesn't work, nudging us closer to what will. Each setback, each stumble, each 'failed' attempt adds a layer of understanding, resilience, and wisdom to our entrepreneurial journey.

Remember, some of the most successful entrepreneurs in history have experienced failure. They have faced disappointments, setbacks, and, at times, colossal failures. But they didn't let these experiences define them. Instead, they used these experiences to redefine their approach, their strategies, and their journey.

Risk and failure, indeed, become part of our journey, our evolution, our story. They are chapters in our book, verses in our song, strokes on our canvas. We may not always like them, we may not always want them, but we learn to respect them, for they offer us more than meets the eye.

Remember that taking risks involves embracing a certain level of vulnerability. It's acknowledging that we don't have all the answers, that we can't predict every outcome, that we don't have a crystal ball to foretell the future. And that's okay. This vulnerability isn't a weakness; it's a strength. It's the strength of being authentic, of being true to ourselves and our journey.

It's also about understanding that each risk we take is a conscious choice. It's a choice to pursue our vision, to follow our passion, to believe in our potential. When we choose to take a risk, we're also choosing to trust ourselves. We're choosing to listen to our intuition, our gut, our inner voice. We're choosing to honor our journey, regardless of the outcome.

Now, let's revisit our understanding of failure. In the entrepreneurial world, we don't perceive failure as a definitive end. We don't see it as a sign to stop, to quit, to give up. No. We see failure as a signal to pause, to reflect, to learn. We see it as a chance to reassess our strategies, to recalibrate our path, to reinvent our approach.

Think of failure as a feedback mechanism. It tells us what isn't working. It shows us where we need to improve, where we need to change, where we need to grow. It's not a badge of shame, but a badge of honor. It's an emblem of our courage to try, our willingness to learn, and our determination to succeed.

Let's also remember that failure doesn't exist in isolation. It exists in relation to our goals, our vision, our aspirations. It's a part of our journey, not the destination. It's a phase, not the finale. It's a moment, not a lifetime.

Embracing risk and reframing failure can be daunting. But let's not forget, every significant achievement in history, every innovation, every breakthrough has been born out of risk and peppered with failures. These elements are not only part of the entrepreneurial journey but part of the human journey.

As we continue exploring the winning entrepreneurial mindset, let's remember that the journey is as important as the destination. And on this journey, every risk we take, every failure we face, is an opportunity to learn, grow, and evolve. So, let's embrace the journey, the risks, the failures, and let's move forward, shall we?

Power of positivity

Power of positivity – those three words embody a force that, in the entrepreneurial world, is as essential as a business plan or a marketing strategy. A positive attitude can be your beacon in the darkest storm, your anchor in turbulent times, and your compass when the path gets unclear. As an entrepreneur, harnessing this power can fuel your journey like nothing else.

Now, it's not about ignoring the reality or shying away from challenges. Positivity isn't about wearing rose-tinted glasses and living in denial. It's about acknowledging the reality but choosing to focus on the silver linings, the opportunities, the potentialities. It's about having a hopeful outlook, an optimistic perspective, a belief in possibilities.

Let's look at optimism. It's not just about expecting good outcomes; it's about working towards them. It's about taking calculated risks, making informed decisions, and then believing in their potential. It's about trusting your abilities, your knowledge, your intuition, and being confident that you can navigate whatever comes your way.

Remember that optimism is like a self-fulfilling prophecy. When you believe in positive outcomes, you're more likely to work diligently towards them. You're more likely to persist in the face of obstacles, bounce back from setbacks, and stay resilient in the face of adversity. You create a positive cycle of belief, action, and result.

Now, let's talk about self-belief. In the entrepreneurial journey, self-belief is your unwavering faith in yourself and your capabilities. It's your conviction that you have the talent, the skills, the passion to turn your vision into reality. It's about knowing your worth, appreciating your strengths, acknowledging your weaknesses, and still saying, "I can do this."

Self-belief empowers you to take risks, to explore new opportunities, to push your boundaries. It fuels your persistence, your resilience, your tenacity. It helps you keep going when times get tough, when doubts creep in, when the road gets rocky. Self-belief is your inner strength, your inner light, your inner guide.

Now, harnessing optimism and self-belief is a conscious choice, a conscious effort. It's about choosing to see the glass half full, choosing to trust yourself, choosing to stay hopeful. It's about turning challenges into opportunities, setbacks into learnings, and fears into growth.

Expanding on the power of positivity, we understand that it is a potent catalyst for change, a force multiplier for your efforts, and a shield against the inevitable setbacks on your entrepreneurial journey. The power of positivity is not just about maintaining a sunny disposition, it is a mindset, a habit, a choice that can dramatically alter the trajectory of your entrepreneurial journey.

Imagine the entrepreneurial journey as a marathon. The path is long, often uphill, and the weather is not always perfect. There will be moments of exhaustion, of doubt, even of pain. Yet, the marathoners who complete the race and reach the finish line are the ones who, despite the hardships, maintain a positive outlook. They embrace the challenge, welcome the effort, and believe in their capacity to endure and succeed. This is the power of positivity in action.

Consider optimism and self-belief as two essential components of this power. Optimism is the torchlight that illuminates the path, even in the darkest of nights. It is the belief that despite the bumps and turns on the road, it will eventually lead you to your destination. It doesn't mean naively believing that everything will go smoothly. Instead, it is trusting in your ability to handle whatever comes your way, knowing that you have the resources and the capability to navigate and negotiate whatever obstacles appear.

On the other hand, self-belief is the fuel that keeps you going. It is the deeply ingrained conviction that you have what it takes to reach your goals. It propels you forward, pushes you to keep going, even when you're out of breath, even when every muscle in your body is screaming for rest. Self-belief doesn't imply arrogance or an inflated sense of self. Instead, it is a genuine acknowledgment of your abilities and potential, backed by a firm commitment to harnessing these to the fullest.

Positivity, optimism, and self-belief also lead to resilience, another crucial trait for any entrepreneur. When you're positive, you're more adaptable, more able to bounce back from setbacks, and less likely to be fazed by obstacles. You see failures as feedback, not as a full stop. You learn from them, adapt, and come back stronger and more determined.

In conclusion, entrepreneurship is adventure filled with ups and downs, successes and failures, and joys and challenges. But, armed with a positive mindset, an optimistic outlook, and unshakeable self-belief, you have the tools you need to navigate this journey successfully. These powerful forces can be your compass, guiding you towards your goal, fueling your journey, and transforming your entrepreneurial dreams into reality. Remember, your mindset determines your approach to everything in life, including entrepreneurship. Cultivate a positive one, and you're well on your way to creating the success you envision. Let's seize the day, embrace the journey, and build the future we desire. Let's power our entrepreneurial journey with positivity!

Conclusion

I cannot overstate the influence and importance of the right mindset in your entrepreneurial journey. The mindset you hold significantly impacts every aspect of your entrepreneurial life – from how you handle failures, to how you approach risks, to how you perceive growth and success. A winning entrepreneurial mindset, therefore, is not just beneficial but essential for every aspirant standing on the threshold of this exciting journey.

Let's take a moment to recapture the journey we've embarked upon in this chapter. We started by exploring the traits of successful entrepreneurs. We delved into their mindsets, dissecting the attitudes, habits, and beliefs that contribute to their successes. We saw how curiosity, perseverance, resilience, and an undying zest for learning typify the entrepreneurial spirit.

Next, we stepped into the arena of growth mindset – understanding that our abilities and intelligence are not fixed, but capable of development. We acknowledged the power of yet, the power of potential, the power of resilience. Embracing this mindset is like acquiring a key that unlocks doors to personal and professional growth, a powerful antidote against stagnation and complacency.

We then ventured into arguably the most daunting aspect of entrepreneurship – the possibility of failure. But rather than shy away from it, we learned to embrace it, reframing it not as an end but as a part of the process. We recognized failure as a teacher, a guide, helping us to recalibrate our actions and hone our strategies.

And finally, we delved into the power of positivity, highlighting the crucial role optimism and self-belief play in fueling your entrepreneurial journey. We realized that a positive outlook can not only keep us going amid challenges but can also transform our perceptions, actions, and outcomes.

But remember, dear reader, a mindset is not something you acquire overnight. It requires conscious effort, regular nurturing, and a willingness to challenge your existing beliefs and assumptions. It's about committing to a journey of continuous learning and growth.

As we turn the page to the next chapter of our entrepreneurial journey, I encourage you to carry with you the lessons we've learned here. Keep them close to your heart. They are not merely ideas to be read and forgotten but principles to be embodied and lived.

The journey of entrepreneurship is an incredible adventure, filled with incredible highs and challenging lows. But equipped with the winning entrepreneurial mindset we've explored in this chapter you are prepared not just to venture but to thrive in this exhilarating landscape. As we forge ahead, let's carry with us the belief that our potential is limitless, our journey is exciting, and our future is bright. Let's embrace the winning entrepreneurial mindset, and let's create the entrepreneurial future we envision.

The path ahead is uncharted, but the potential for success is profound. So, let's continue with optimism, grit, and an unwavering belief in our capabilities. Remember, every step taken with the winning entrepreneurial mindset is a step toward success. Let's step boldly into the unknown, armed with our indomitable entrepreneurial mindset, ready to conquer the world!

Questions

Welcome to the next segment of our journey, a set of thought-provoking questions. They're here to help you delve deeper into your understanding of the principles laid out in Chapter 5: The Winning Entrepreneurial Mindset. They are not mere questions, but tools to help you introspect, reflect, and build an entrepreneurial mindset that is armed with resilience, positivity, and an unwavering belief in your capabilities. Embrace these questions with honesty and openness and see the transformation they can spark in your entrepreneurial journey.

1. What are some key traits you believe define a successful entrepreneur? How do these align with your own traits and qualities?

2. Can you recall a moment where a growth mindset helped you overcome a personal or professional challenge?

3. How do you view failure? Do you see it as a setback or as an opportunity for learning and growth?

4. In what ways have you practiced resilience in your life? How can you further strengthen this quality?

5. How does positivity influence your daily life and decisions? Can you share an example of when optimism helped you during a difficult time?

6. When faced with risk, what is your typical reaction? Do you embrace it, or do you shy away from it?

7. How can you reinforce the traits of a successful entrepreneurial mindset in your daily routine?

Remember, there are no right or wrong answers. What matters is that you're willing to explore and engage with these questions, making them an integral part of your journey towards a winning entrepreneurial mindset. Enjoy the process of discovery, and let it shape your path towards entrepreneurial success.

Exercises

Welcome to this integral part of your entrepreneurial journey – the exercises. These exercises are designed to help you actively cultivate and strengthen the mindset that makes for successful entrepreneurship. They go beyond being mere activities; consider them as catalysts that will speed up your progress towards becoming a winning entrepreneur. Be committed and approach them with the mindset of growth, learning, and adaptability.

1. **Trait Tracking:** Make a list of the traits you believe successful entrepreneurs possess. Next to each trait, write down one action you can take daily to cultivate that trait in yourself.

2. **Failure Analysis:** Think of a time you faced failure. Write a reflection about what you learned from that experience, how it helped you grow, and how it could be reframed as an opportunity.

3. **Risk-Taking Journal:** For a week, record each time you take a risk, no matter how small. Write about what you learned, how you felt, and how you can apply these lessons in the future.

4. **Positivity Diary:** Each day, write down three positive things that happened. Reflect on how they made you feel and why they happened.

5. **Growth Visualization:** Spend 10 minutes each day visualizing yourself as a successful entrepreneur.

Focus on the traits you possess and how they contribute to your success.

6. **Resilience Builder:** Think of a challenging situation you're currently facing. Write down three strategies you can use to navigate through this situation effectively.

7. **Affirmation Practice:** Write down three affirmations that embody the entrepreneurial traits you wish to strengthen. Repeat these affirmations to yourself every morning and night.

Remember, the real value of these exercises lies in your willingness to commit to them and see them through. They are your tools for self-improvement and growth, aiding you to shape a mindset that not only understands but lives and breathes entrepreneurship. Enjoy this journey of personal development and watch as it transforms your entrepreneurial journey!

Affirmation

Creating and using affirmations can be a powerful tool to reinforce the positive mindset that is so integral to successful entrepreneurship. This affirmation is specifically designed to encapsulate the essence of Chapter 5: The Winning Entrepreneurial Mindset. It's designed to serve as a daily reminder of your commitment to growth, resilience, positivity, and the embracing of risk and failure as vital parts of your journey.

Here's your affirmation:

"I am a resilient and positive entrepreneur. I embrace learning and adaptability, turning risks into opportunities. I view failures as steppingstones towards success and believe in the power of my entrepreneurial journey."

Every time you repeat this affirmation, let each word sink in, visualize yourself embodying these traits, and believe in its truth. Start your day with it, remind yourself of it during your lows, and let it be your last thought before sleeping. This affirmation is your companion, your mantra, guiding you on your path to becoming a winning entrepreneur. Embrace it and let its power permeate your thoughts and actions.

> "I've learned that you can't have everything and do everything at the same time."
> - Oprah Winfrey

Chapter Six:
Building the Balance Bridge- Work-Life Harmony

In the quiet hours of the early morning, with a hot cup of coffee in my hand, I find myself reflecting on the journey we've taken together so far. As I look out at the golden hues of dawn streaking across the sky, it's not the various facets of entrepreneurship that weigh on my mind. Instead, it's the precarious dance we perform daily - the balancing act between our work, our passions, and the many other aspects of our lives.

As we step into this new phase, let's take a moment to recognize that it is a journey. Often, in our quest for success, we overlook the importance of striking a balance. It's not unusual, I assure you. However, to sustain the long race that is entrepreneurship, it's essential we learn to create harmony between our work and life.

Harmony is a more accurate and forgiving term than balance. It represents a state where all components exist in a beautiful synergy, a fluid state where different parts of our lives seamlessly integrate with each other, much like a well-orchestrated symphony. This chapter is about nurturing that harmony, enabling us to be successful entrepreneurs without letting our work overshadow the other enriching aspects of our lives.

We'll dive into understanding the nature of work-life harmony and why it's crucial, especially for entrepreneurs. We will learn how to recognize the signs of imbalance and explore strategies to address them. Together, we'll celebrate the wins and navigate through the rough patches, all while maintaining a joyful rhythm between our work and life.

Remember, there are no shortcuts here, just like entrepreneurship itself. But fret not, with each step we take, we are moving closer to finding our unique harmony. After all, at the end of the day, aren't we all trying to build a life that sings in perfect harmony, a life that is not just successful but also meaningful and fulfilling? Let's embark on this journey to find that melody. It's time to build our balance bridge.

Work-Life Balance

When it comes to entrepreneurship, we often find ourselves consumed by our work. The lines between work and personal life become blurred, creating a cycle that leaves us perpetually caught in the whirlwind of business tasks, meetings, brainstorming sessions, and whatnot. The concept of work-life balance is crucial, but it tends to be one of the most misunderstood.

Work-life balance, dear reader, is not an elusive, ideal state of perfect equilibrium, where we're able to allocate an exact, equal amount of time to our personal and professional lives. Instead, it is the ability to fluidly manage the commitments and activities in our lives, to ensure a sense of fulfillment and satisfaction across all domains. It's about ensuring that our work fuels us, instead of depleting us, and that our personal life is enriching, rather than serving as a mere break from work.

The significance of maintaining a healthy work-life balance cannot be overstated. First and foremost, it enhances our overall wellbeing. By creating room for activities and relationships that bring us joy and relaxation, we can mitigate stress, prevent burnout, and promote mental and emotional health. Furthermore, it contributes to increased productivity and innovation. When we have time to recharge and refresh our minds, we can approach our work with renewed energy, creative ideas, and a greater sense of motivation.

Contrary to what we may think, work-life balance is not a luxury; it's an absolute necessity. Just as we need to refuel a car to keep it running efficiently, we need to ensure that we are looking after our own well-being to sustain the demanding journey of entrepreneurship. A lack of balance can lead to fatigue, diminished focus, and lower work quality, not to mention the potential damage to our relationships and personal life.

As we navigate deeper into the sea of work-life balance, we realize that achieving this equilibrium is not about perfection, but about making continuous progress towards a balanced lifestyle. The idea of 'balance' might differ for each individual, influenced by a myriad of factors like career stage, personal circumstances, and individual aspirations. This is why it's important to reflect and understand what balance means to us personally, and then move towards creating that.

When we speak of a 'balanced lifestyle,' we're referring to an existence where we're able to successfully juggle our professional commitments without compromising on the facets of life that bring us joy and relaxation. It doesn't necessarily mean working less, but it does mean working smart. It's about managing our energy, not just our time.

As entrepreneurs, we are fuelled by passion, determination, and the thrill of creating something of our own. This energy propels us forward, but without proper management, it can also lead us to overextend ourselves. Hence, energy management becomes a critical part of work-life balance. By becoming aware of our energy cycles, we can schedule our tasks accordingly. Tackling challenging tasks when our energy levels are high and scheduling downtime when they are low can help us maximize productivity without feeling drained.

Understanding work-life balance also entails acknowledging that not all hours are created equal. There will be times when our business needs more attention, and times when our personal life will require more of our time and energy. During product launches or crucial negotiations, our work might necessitate more focus. In contrast, personal events or situations like family emergencies, holidays, or self-care times will require us to step back from work. Being flexible and adaptable to these changing dynamics is a part of maintaining a healthy work-life equilibrium.

In our quest for balance, we mustn't forget that 'life' is not a single, homogenous entity. It's a beautiful tapestry woven from various threads - family, health, friendships, hobbies, personal growth, spirituality, and more. Ensuring work-life balance means not neglecting any of these aspects. We need to be vigilant about giving ourselves the opportunity to unwind, to be with loved ones, to pursue a hobby, or just to relax and do nothing at all.

Creating and maintaining a healthy work-life balance is a dynamic process. It requires continuous effort, a willingness to evolve, and the courage to make tough decisions when needed. But remember, the objective here is not to add another chore to your already overflowing to-do list. Instead, it's about paving the path to a more fulfilling, content, and joyful life.

As we continue this exploration, we'll delve into practical strategies to cultivate this balance, prioritize our well-being, and craft an entrepreneurial journey that is as fulfilling and enriching personally as it is professionally. Let's remember that we're striving for a balance that gives us the best of both worlds, allowing us to be successful entrepreneurs without compromising on our happiness and well-being. Let's embark on this path of harmony, living our lives to the fullest, in every possible sense.

Practical strategies for balance

In crafting our personal masterpiece of work-life harmony, practical strategies are our brushes, allowing us to paint a vibrant picture of balance. Let's delve into the art of implementing habits and practices that enable us to construct a more harmonious lifestyle.

Creating boundaries between our work and personal life is a foundational practice. Boundaries need not be rigid walls; they can be flexible, adaptable lines that respect our need for work and rest. As entrepreneurs, we might have the luxury of setting our work hours, but this can often lead to work creeping into our personal time. A good habit here would be setting clear work hours and adhering to them. When we're at work, we give it our all, and when we're off, we disconnect completely.

Next, let's talk about the power of 'no.' The word 'no' can be incredibly liberating. It's about understanding that our time and energy are finite resources and saying 'no' to what doesn't serve our purpose or bring us joy. As entrepreneurs, we will often come across opportunities and requests that, while tempting or flattering, may not align with our goals or may drain our energy disproportionately. Developing the ability to say 'no' in such situations is a valuable skill that can greatly contribute to our work-life balance.

Another strategy is to master the art of delegation. Entrepreneurship often feels like a solitary journey, but it doesn't have to be. By learning to delegate effectively, we can free up our time to focus on tasks that require our unique skills and attention, while empowering our team members to grow and contribute.

Prioritization is also a key strategy for balance. Not all tasks are created equal, understanding this can make a world of difference in how we manage our time and energy. The Pareto principle, also known as the 80/20 rule, states that 80% of the effects come from 20% of the causes. Applying this rule in our work-life scenario, we focus on the 20% tasks that will create 80% of the value, allowing us to work more efficiently.

Self-care deserves a special mention when we talk about maintaining balance. It's not just about spa days or vacations, although those are certainly enjoyable. It's about creating a lifestyle that allows us to replenish our physical, mental, and emotional energy regularly. This could mean developing a fitness routine, practicing mindfulness, indulging in a hobby, or just taking out time each day to relax and do nothing.

Next, I want to talk about the practice of gratitude. In the hustle of work and life, it's easy to lose sight of our accomplishments and blessings. Making it a habit to recognize and appreciate what's going well in our lives can give us a sense of contentment and motivate us to continue striving for balance.

As we navigate this vibrant journey of balancing our professional and personal lives, it is crucial to understand that this balance is not a fixed state but rather a dynamic equilibrium. The scales might tip one way or another depending on our current circumstances and goals. Recognizing this is key to prevent us from being overly hard on ourselves when things don't seem perfectly aligned. Being adaptive and proactive is part of this process, and it helps us fine-tune our work-life harmony over time.

Time management is one skill that plays an essential role in maintaining this equilibrium. Often, we might find ourselves overwhelmed with tasks, but if we look closely, we might realize that the issue is not the lack of time, but rather how we manage it. Learning to organize our day, creating a task list, and setting realistic deadlines can help us be more productive without encroaching on our personal time.

Moreover, adopting a positive outlook towards the challenges that come our way can help us view them as opportunities for growth rather than hindrances. This does not mean ignoring the stress or pretending that everything is perfect. It is about acknowledging the situation, understanding its implications, and then focusing on the steps we can take to improve it.

Work-life harmony is also about cherishing the relationships we have. Our connections with family, friends, and even colleagues can serve as a refreshing counterpoint to our work, providing emotional support and happiness. So, carving out time for our loved ones and nurturing these relationships is a vital aspect of maintaining balance.

On a final note, it is crucial to understand that maintaining work-life balance doesn't necessarily mean equal allocation of time to work and personal life. It's about being present in whatever we are doing at a given moment and deriving satisfaction from it. When we are working, we are fully committed to our tasks, and when we are resting or pursuing our hobbies, we are entirely in that moment, savoring the joy and relaxation it brings. The essence of work-life harmony lies in this immersive experience, this mindful existence.

In the end, remember that it is okay to not have it all figured out. Sometimes, the equilibrium might get disturbed, and we might find ourselves leaning towards one aspect of our lives more than the other. It is during these times that the strategies we discussed come to our aid, helping us realign and find our balance again. Building work-life harmony is a conscious, continuous process - a beautiful dance between our aspirations and our well-being. As we keep dancing, let's remember to enjoy the music along the way.

Real-life stories of women entrepreneurs

In this journey of exploring the building of the balance bridge, it would be beneficial to look at real-life examples. Stories of women who, like many of us, have navigated their path and have found their equilibrium. Not in a way that means balance in every moment, but as a means of creating a dynamic harmony over time.

I recall the journey of Emily, a thriving software entrepreneur. She was a mother of two young kids and a successful CEO of a burgeoning tech start-up. At first glance, it seemed like she was doing it all effortlessly, but as we spoke, she opened about the challenges she faced in maintaining work-life harmony.

For Emily, the turning point came when she realized that it wasn't about having it all, but having what mattered the most. She identified her non-negotiables, both at work and home, and focused on them. She became more comfortable with delegating tasks, both to her team at work and to her partner at home. She introduced flexibility into her work structure, sometimes working late into the night when the kids were asleep, sometimes taking half a day off to attend her daughter's school event. The essential insight from Emily's journey is about prioritizing and letting go of the pursuit of perfection.

Let's also consider the example of Lily, a prolific writer and entrepreneur. Lily had always been a night owl, her creativity sparked most in the quiet of the night. But this schedule became challenging when she started her content creation agency and had to align with her clients' conventional working hours. The stress was taking a toll on her health and personal life.

In her quest for balance, Lily restructured her business model. She started outsourcing some of her tasks to freelancers in different time zones, which allowed her to get back to her natural rhythm. She also started practicing mindfulness meditation to reduce stress. For Lily, the key was to honor her natural tendencies and find creative solutions that accommodated those tendencies.

These stories demonstrate that there is no 'one size fits all' solution to achieving work-life harmony. It's a personal journey that requires self-awareness, adaptability, and above all, compassion for oneself. Each woman entrepreneur weaves her tapestry of balance, embedded with unique experiences, priorities, and coping strategies.

Let us take inspiration from these stories but remember that our journey towards building work-life harmony will be distinct and personalized. There will be trials and errors, adjustments, and readjustments. But with every step, we will be learning, growing, and inching closer to our unique work-life equilibrium.

Mental wellness in entrepreneurship

As we delve deeper into our journey towards work-life harmony, I find it imperative to address an aspect that's often neglected in the hustle and bustle of entrepreneurship—mental wellness. Many of us, especially as women entrepreneurs, can get so caught up in our business ventures and personal commitments that we forget to care for ourselves. But as the saying goes, "you can't pour from an empty cup."

Mental wellness is not a luxury; it's a necessity, an integral part of our journey towards balance. It's about acknowledging that our minds, like our bodies, need rest and care. It's about understanding that our mental state can significantly impact our productivity, creativity, and the overall quality of our lives.

To embrace the entrepreneurial journey fully, we must give mental wellness the importance it deserves. It is a vital part of our toolkit to maintain balance amidst the varying demands of our lives. We must acknowledge that self-care is not selfish—it's the fuel that keeps our engine running smoothly.

How do we incorporate mental wellness into our entrepreneurial lives, you might wonder? It begins with recognizing that every small step towards self-care counts. Taking a five-minute break from your laptop to stretch and breathe deeply, going for a short walk outdoors, or simply enjoying a cup of tea in silence—all these seemingly tiny acts can significantly impact our mental wellbeing.

It's also about setting healthy boundaries—knowing when to switch off the work mode and attend to our personal needs and wants. It's about understanding that it's okay not to answer that email right away, it's okay to take a day off when you're feeling overwhelmed—it's okay to put your mental wellness first.

Entrepreneurship is often seen as a race, where speed and constant activity are glorified. But I invite you to see it as a marathon instead, where endurance, resilience, and pacing oneself are crucial for reaching the finish line. And in this marathon, mental wellness is not a pit stop; it's the track on which we run.

Another significant aspect of mental wellness is seeking help when needed. It's about breaking the stigma around mental health and understanding that reaching out to a mental health professional is a sign of strength, not weakness.

Remember, it's not just about building a successful business; it's about leading a fulfilling life. And for that, we must give our minds the care and attention they deserve. We must build our balance bridge, not just between work and life but also between our external commitments and internal wellbeing.

As we navigate our entrepreneurial journey, let us remember to carry along our mental wellness. For it's not the destination but the journey that matters. And it's up to us to make this journey balanced, fulfilling, and joyous.

In expanding further, I'd like to note that mental wellness is as much about what we don't do as what we do. It's about learning to say 'no' when we need to. It's about understanding that we can't do everything for everyone. It's about appreciating our value and worth, and not feeling guilty about making time for ourselves.

It's vital to remember that we, as entrepreneurs, are our most important asset. If we don't care for ourselves, how can we expect to care for our businesses and those who depend on us? It's like the safety instructions on an airplane: "Put on your own oxygen mask before assisting others." To be the most effective in our roles, we need to prioritize our own mental wellness.

Practicing mindfulness can be a wonderful tool to maintain our mental wellness. Being present in the moment helps us better understand ourselves, our needs, and our emotions. It allows us to respond rather than react to stressful situations, helping maintain a sense of balance.

Journaling can also be a powerful tool. Pouring out our thoughts and emotions on paper can be therapeutic. It can help us gain perspective, recognize patterns, and understand our feelings better. It's like having a conversation with ourselves, a conversation that can lead to a deeper understanding and appreciation of our journey.

Similarly, cultivating gratitude can significantly impact our mental wellness. It's about recognizing and appreciating the positives in our lives - no matter how big or small. It's about shifting our focus from what's going wrong to what's going right. It's amazing how this simple shift in perspective can uplift our mood and mindset.

I'd also encourage us to embrace the idea of a "mental wellness day"—a day to rest, rejuvenate, and recharge. A day where work emails are off-limits, and the focus is on self-care. After all, we need to maintain a balance between our professional ambitions and personal needs.

Lastly, remember, it's perfectly okay to seek help. Just as we consult a doctor for physical ailments, consulting a mental health professional for our mental wellbeing should be normalized. There's no bravery in suffering in silence.

Real strength lies in acknowledging our struggles and seeking the help we need.

The entrepreneurial journey can be challenging, but with the right tools, it's a journey we can navigate with balance, strength, and grace. As we step into the next phase of our journey, let us remember to bring along our mental wellness. Let's remember that we are not alone, and it's okay to pause, breathe, and take care of ourselves.

So, dear entrepreneur, as we venture further, let's pledge to not just work smart, but live wisely. Let's remember to build the bridge of balance, not just between work and life, but also between doing and being, achieving and appreciating, dreaming, and living. Because that's where true success lies—in the harmony of our professional achievements and personal wellbeing.

Conclusion

As we near the end of this chapter, it's essential to remember that the idea of work-life balance isn't a destination, but a journey—a constant dance of give and take, of push and pull. It's a process that demands intentionality and mindfulness, a journey that challenges us to maintain equilibrium amidst the waves of our entrepreneurial ambitions and personal lives.

You see, striving for balance isn't about reaching some utopic state of perfect harmony between work and life. Rather, it's about recognizing when things are tipping too much in one direction and taking the steps necessary to steer back towards center. It's about accepting that there will be days where work demands more of our attention, and that's okay. Equally, there will be times where our personal life requires us to step back from work, and that's okay too.

Work-life balance is about fluidity and flexibility. It's about knowing that each day might look different, and that's a part of the journey. It's about the daily, conscious choices we make to give ourselves the compassion and grace we often extend to others.

Let's remember that we're not just entrepreneurs, but also individuals—with dreams, desires, relationships, hobbies, and passions that extend beyond the sphere of our businesses. Let's cherish and nurture these aspects of our lives, for they add to our wholeness and enrich our entrepreneurial journeys.

I urge you to take a moment to envision your ideal balance bridge. What does it look like? What practices do you need to implement to maintain it? Take time to reflect on these questions, sketch out your bridge, and hold yourself accountable to take those steps.

Realize that it's okay to prioritize yourself. It's okay to set boundaries. It's okay to take a break. It's okay to say no when you need to. It's okay to seek help. It's more than okay, it's necessary—for your wellbeing and for the long-term sustainability of your entrepreneurial dreams.

I want you to know that it's within your power to construct your balance bridge, to create a life where your work fuels your passion, and your passion enriches your life. But remember, it's a constant process of tuning and retuning, of adjusting and readjusting.

So, dear entrepreneur, as you turn the page to the next chapter, remember that you have the power to build your balance bridge. Remember that you deserve a fulfilling professional life without sacrificing your personal happiness and wellbeing. You have the power to create a work-life harmony that resonates with your unique rhythm. It's your journey, your bridge, and your balance.

Onwards to the journey, my friend. Let's embrace the adventure that is entrepreneurship, remembering to cherish each moment, celebrate each victory, learn from each setback, and nurture the balance that leads to a fulfilling, enriching, and successful journey.

Questions

It's now time to reflect deeper on your own understanding and thoughts about work-life harmony as we've explored it in Chapter 6: Building the Balance Bridge. Remember, introspection and self-evaluation are crucial steps towards growth and improvement. Your answers to these questions can help you understand your current work-life dynamics better and highlight the areas where you might want to implement changes. Let these questions guide you in your journey towards finding your unique work-life harmony.

1. How would you currently rate your work-life balance? What specific elements contribute to your satisfaction or dissatisfaction?

2. What habits or practices do you currently have in place that promote work-life balance? Are there any new habits you'd like to cultivate?

3. Are there any specific challenges or obstacles that prevent you from achieving a better work-life balance? How might you address these obstacles?

4. How does your current work-life balance affect your mental health and overall wellbeing?

5. What specific actions will you take in the short-term (next few weeks) and in the long-term (next few months to a year) to improve your work-life harmony?

6. How can you ensure that you're giving sufficient time and attention to your personal life while still staying committed to your entrepreneurial journey?

7. Reflect on the case studies discussed in this chapter. How can their experiences inform your own journey towards work-life harmony?

These questions might prompt you to explore some deep and perhaps challenging aspects of your life. That's okay. Remember, it's through exploring these challenges that we often find our most profound growth and change. So, take your time, be honest with yourself, and let these questions guide you towards building your own balance bridge.

Exercises

We've journeyed through the essence of work-life harmony in Chapter 6, and now it's time to turn that understanding into action. The exercises provided here are practical activities designed to help you implement a healthier work-life balance. Remember, the path to balance is not a sprint, but a marathon that involves continuous efforts, adjustments, and introspection.

1. **Work-Life Balance Audit:** Dedicate some time to carefully analyze your current work-life balance. Break down your daily activities into categories (work, family, leisure, self-care, etc.) and calculate the percentage of time you spend on each. Reflect on whether you're satisfied with this distribution or if there are areas you'd like to adjust.

2. **The "No" Practice:** Learning to say "no" is an important aspect of maintaining work-life balance. For a week, practice saying "no" to tasks or engagements that you feel are not contributing positively to your work-life harmony or are creating unnecessary stress. Reflect on how this impacts your time and energy.

3. **Self-Care Plan:** Create a self-care plan that includes activities you enjoy and that contribute to your well-being. These can include physical activities, hobbies, mindfulness practices, and more. Make sure to dedicate some time to these activities each day, no matter how busy your schedule may be.

4. **Mental Health Check-ins:** Regularly monitor your mental health state. This could be done through journaling your thoughts and feelings or using mental health apps that guide you through self-check processes. If you feel overwhelmed, seek professional help.

5. **Set Boundaries:** Define your working hours and stick to them as much as possible. Communicate these boundaries clearly to your colleagues and clients. The same goes for your personal time. Ensure you have uninterrupted personal time where work does not intrude.

6. **Delegate and Outsource:** Identify tasks that can be delegated or outsourced. This is a crucial step to freeing up some of your time and reducing your stress levels.

7. **Reflection and Adjustment:** At the end of each week, reflect on your work-life balance. What worked well? What didn't? What changes can you make in the coming week? Make necessary adjustments and continue to refine your approach to achieving work-life harmony.

Take these exercises at your own pace, and don't be hard on yourself if you find it challenging at first. The goal is to gradually create a routine and lifestyle that respects both your professional ambitions and personal needs. So go ahead, invest your time and energy in these exercises, and pave the way to a balanced and fulfilling entrepreneurial journey!

Affirmation

Affirmations are a powerful tool for building the mindset that supports work-life harmony. By regularly repeating an uplifting and empowering statement, you're reinforcing the belief in your ability to achieve a balanced life, and creating a positive mental environment that nourishes your well-being.

Here's your affirmation for Chapter 6: Building the Balance Bridge: Work-Life Harmony:

"I acknowledge and honor the importance of balance in my life. I am fully capable of managing my work and personal life in harmony. Each day, I make conscious choices that nurture my well-being and fuel my success. I embrace the flexibility to adjust and adapt, knowing that every step I take brings me closer to the balanced life I desire and deserve."

Repeat this affirmation at least once every day, ideally at the start of your day or during your moments of self-care. Believe in the words you're saying and visualize yourself living them. Remember, affirmations are not just about the words, but the emotions and belief behind them. So say it, feel it, believe it, and witness the transformation towards a balanced life unfold.

"It takes a tribe to build a successful business. Surround yourself with people who believe in you."
- Barbara Corcoran

Chapter Seven:
Building Your Tribe

As we journey further into the world of entrepreneurship, we'll be exploring another integral aspect, one that holds the power to either make or break your venture—your tribe.

In entrepreneurship and in life, the people we surround ourselves with have a profound impact on us. They influence our thoughts, our actions, our successes, and even our failures. They can lift us to new heights or drag us down into the trenches of despair. That's why it's so crucial to choose our tribe wisely, and to build it with intention, care, and mutual respect.

The essence of a tribe in entrepreneurship isn't just about the number of people in your network. It's not just about having a massive LinkedIn following or hundreds of contacts on your phone. It's about the quality of these connections, the mutual respect, the shared visions, and the reciprocal support.

Building a tribe—your tribe—is a deeply personal endeavor. It is about creating a network of relationships that nourish you, challenge you, and push you towards your highest potential. It is about building bridges and fostering connections that fuel your passion, ignite your entrepreneurial spirit, and root you in your mission.

So, why is this tribe so critical? The answer is simple. We, as humans, are inherently social beings. We thrive on connection, on being a part of something bigger than ourselves. In the entrepreneurial landscape, this collective 'something bigger' is your tribe. Your tribe is the powerhouse that fuels your ideas, strengthens your resolve, and buoys your spirits in times of challenge. Your tribe is not just your network; it's your support system, your sounding board, your cheering squad.

Remember, your tribe is not about creating an echo chamber where everyone shares the same ideas and viewpoints. Rather, it's about gathering a diverse group of people who offer different perspectives, insights, and experiences that can enrich your entrepreneurial journey. These individuals will challenge your thinking, inspire innovative ideas, and motivate you to push beyond your comfort zone. They will celebrate your victories and help you navigate your failures.

And, just as importantly, your tribe is about reciprocity. It's not only about what you can gain from others, but also about what you can offer them in return. It's about mutual growth, mutual support, and mutual success. It's about creating a culture of generosity, where knowledge, experiences, and resources are shared freely.

Now, the question arises: how do we build this tribe? Like any worthwhile endeavor, it begins with clarity. You need to be clear about your vision, your values, and your venture. Once you have that clarity, you can start seeking out individuals who align with your mission and resonate with your passion.

As we move through this chapter, we'll be delving into the nuts and bolts of tribe building. We'll look at different strategies to identify, connect, and cultivate relationships with the individuals who can add value to your entrepreneurial journey. From leveraging digital platforms to fostering connections in real life, we'll explore a myriad of avenues to build your tribe.

And, remember, tribe-building is not an overnight process. It's a continual journey of fostering and nurturing connections. It's about quality over quantity, depth over breadth. Be patient with the process and be genuine in your interactions. After all, at its core, building your tribe is about human connection. It's about building bridges of mutual respect, understanding, and support. So, let's continue this journey together, as we delve deeper into the art of building your tribe, your entrepreneurial powerhouse.

The power of networking

Now, networking is a term you've probably heard countless times before in various contexts. It's been heralded as a vital component of career advancement, personal growth, and, of course, entrepreneurial success. Yet, the term has somehow garnered a reputation as something cold, sterile, and transactional. But nothing could be further from the truth.

When approached correctly, networking is an organic, dynamic process of building genuine relationships based on mutual respect, trust, and shared interests. These relationships form the foundation of your tribe, your entrepreneurial powerhouse. They're the connections that will open new opportunities, catalyze innovative ideas, and provide support during challenging times.

The business world is intertwined in countless complex ways, and the connections you make can be the catalyst for unprecedented growth and opportunities. These connections could lead to partnerships, mentorships, or even friendships that become integral to your personal and professional growth. And that's the true power of networking—it transcends the transactional to become transformational.

The benefits of networking are indeed plentiful. But it's not just about meeting people and exchanging business cards. It's about actively fostering and nurturing these connections, about offering and receiving value in a mutually beneficial relationship. It's about being genuinely interested in the other person, their work, their ideas, their passions. It's about listening and learning, about engaging in meaningful conversations that lead to fruitful collaborations.

And in the age of digital connection, networking has become more accessible and expansive than ever before. Social media platforms, professional networking sites, virtual meetups, webinars, online forums—these are all avenues to connect with like-minded individuals from all corners of the world. They enable you to engage with thought leaders in your industry, collaborate with peers, and connect with potential mentors or partners.

Remember, networking is not a one-size-fits-all strategy. It's a personalized process that depends on your individual goals, your industry, your personality. You must find the methods that work best for you. Maybe you thrive in the fast-paced environment of networking events. Or perhaps you prefer the more intimate setting of one-on-one coffee meetings. Maybe you enjoy the convenience and scope of online networking. Whichever avenue you choose, the key is to be authentic, open, and receptive.

The beauty of networking lies in its potential to surprise you, to take you down paths you never anticipated, to introduce you to people who will change your perspective and, in doing so, may alter the trajectory of your entrepreneurial journey. Every conversation, every encounter, is an opportunity for something remarkable.

And let's be clear, networking doesn't imply an insincere or manipulative approach where the goal is solely to extract value. On the contrary, it's about fostering relationships based on authenticity, respect, and mutual support. The most meaningful connections are often those where both parties are invested in each other's success and are ready to extend help when needed.

In this context, let's remember that every interaction is a chance to learn and grow. Engage with others from a place of curiosity, open-mindedness, and genuine interest. Listen attentively, empathize, share your experiences and knowledge. After all, each one of us carries a unique world within us, and the opportunity to peek into someone else's world is a gift not to be squandered.

Moreover, understand that building a robust network doesn't happen overnight. It takes time, patience, and consistent effort. It's like planting a garden—you must consistently water the seeds, provide enough sunlight, remove the weeds, and patiently wait as the plants grow and blossom. Similarly, networking is about planting the seeds of connection, nurturing them with regular interaction, and patiently allowing the relationship to evolve and grow organically.

As you continue to expand your network, you'll find that it begins to function as a vibrant ecosystem, where each connection is linked to the others in intricate and fascinating ways. You might find connections leading to opportunities you had never considered, insights that profoundly change your approach, or collaboration that takes your business to new heights. The potential is truly boundless.

And here's another beautiful aspect of networking - the ability to pay it forward. As you grow and succeed in your journey, you can leverage your network to support others who are starting on their path. You can share your knowledge, make introductions, offer advice. You can become the guide for others that you once sought, and in doing so, you'll find that the cycle of networking continues, creating a ripple effect of support and growth.

In this interconnected world, networking is undoubtedly a superpower for any entrepreneur. It equips you with the resources, support, and opportunities needed to navigate the thrilling, sometimes challenging, journey of entrepreneurship. So, embrace networking, cultivate your tribe, and remember—every connection you make is a new chapter in your entrepreneurial story, a story that is uniquely and beautifully yours.

Finding your Mentors and Role Models

In the grand canvas of your entrepreneurial journey, mentors, and role models function as the guiding stars, lighting the path ahead and offering invaluable insights derived from their own experiences. They've trodden the path you're on, stumbled over obstacles you might encounter, and found ways to navigate through. They've celebrated victories, learned from failures, and have gathered a treasure trove of wisdom along the way.

Let me share with you how I have personally found mentors and role models to be indispensable allies on my entrepreneurial journey. I remember a time when I was grappling with a particularly complex business challenge. I felt lost, unsure of how to move forward. I reached out to a mentor, someone who had not just built successful businesses, but had also weathered storms like the one I was facing. I explained my situation and sought his advice. He listened, asked questions, shared his insights, and gently guided me towards a solution, never imposing his ideas but allowing me space to understand and decide. This was just one of the many instances when I realized the true value of having a mentor.

Role models play a slightly different, yet equally significant role. They inspire you, setting the bar high and showing what's possible. They might be pioneers in your industry, leaders whose values you admire, or simply individuals who've demonstrated exceptional grit and resilience. You may not have direct contact with your role models, but their stories, their journey can profoundly influence your mindset and your approach to entrepreneurship.

Remember, in seeking mentors or role models, it's not just about their success but about their journey—the challenges they've overcome, the values they've upheld, the learning they've gleaned. These are the elements you want to learn from, these are the elements that can truly enhance your entrepreneurial journey.

And how do you find these mentors and role models? Start with your network. Reach out to people who inspire you, ask for advice, or request a casual conversation. Attend industry events, join relevant communities online and offline. Don't hesitate to express your admiration and your desire to learn.

As you engage with potential mentors and role models, it's essential to approach these relationships with a sense of openness and a genuine desire to learn. This is not about imposing your ideas or seeking validation for your choices. It's about understanding their perspectives, learning from their experiences, and growing from their wisdom. It's about fostering a mindset of curiosity, humility, and respect.

In this context, it's also crucial to clarify the nature of the relationship right from the start. Are you looking for a long-term mentorship, periodic guidance, or just a one-time conversation? Are you looking for hands-on support with your business, or are you seeking more strategic guidance? Clearly expressing your expectations and understanding theirs is key to a productive relationship.

Remember, mentors and role models are not there to provide you with ready-made answers. Instead, they serve as a sounding board, helping you refine your thoughts, challenge your assumptions, and arrive at your own decisions. It's not about mimicking their journey, but about deriving insights that can enhance your own.

When I think of my entrepreneurial journey, I realize how much I've learned not just from the successes of my mentors and role models, but also from their failures. They've taught me that every setback is a setup for a comeback, that every failure is a steppingstone to success. They've taught me to embrace my mistakes, to see them as opportunities for learning, and to persist in the face of adversity.

As you engage with your mentors and role models, remember to also give back. Share your insights, your experiences, and your learning. Contribute to the community and help others on their journey. After all, as you rise, lift others too.

Building your tribe of mentors and role models is not a one-time exercise. It's an ongoing process of building relationships, learning, and growing together. It's about fostering a community that supports, inspires, and motivates each other.

So, as you embark on this exciting journey of entrepreneurship, remember to surround yourself with mentors and role models. Reach out, connect, learn, and grow. Your tribe awaits you! And as you grow, you'll discover that you too can become a mentor and role model for others, continuing the cycle of learning and growth, and enriching the entrepreneurial ecosystem.

Empowering others

To step into the fullness of our power is a transformative journey, a journey that is not just about our individual growth but also about the impact we can have on those around us. When we empower ourselves, we gain the strength to empower others, and in doing so, we create a ripple effect that extends far beyond our immediate sphere of influence. Nowhere is this more poignant than in the world of entrepreneurship, especially for us women entrepreneurs.

As we rise, we have the profound opportunity to use our journey, our success, to uplift and inspire other women who are embarking on their entrepreneurial path. Our stories, our experiences, and our insights can serve as the guiding light for their journey, fueling their courage, amplifying their resilience, and igniting their spirit of innovation.

Empowering others isn't about creating carbon copies of our success; rather, it's about fostering an environment where aspiring women entrepreneurs can grow into the best versions of themselves. It's about sharing our learnings, our strategies, and, importantly, our challenges, so they can navigate their own entrepreneurial journey with a greater degree of clarity, confidence, and courage.

Let's look at this concept through a different lens. Imagine a garden filled with various plants. Each plant is unique, each has its own needs, and each contributes to the overall beauty and diversity of the garden. As entrepreneurs, we are the seasoned gardeners sharing our knowledge with the new seedlings. We offer our wisdom on how to navigate the seasons, manage the storms, and bask in the sun. However, we also understand that each seedling must grow in its own way, reflecting its unique strengths and beauty.

In the same vein, when we empower others, we need to honor and respect their individuality. We must encourage them to carve their unique entrepreneurial path, one that aligns with their values, leverages their strengths, and fulfills their vision. Our role is to serve as their mentors, their guides, not their mold.

It's also important to remember that empowerment isn't a one-way street. When we empower others, we too are empowered. Every interaction, every conversation is an opportunity for us to learn, grow, and evolve. As we share our wisdom, we open ourselves up to receive fresh perspectives, innovative ideas, and new insights, further enriching our entrepreneurial journey.

As I reflect further, it becomes increasingly clear that the power to empower others is one of the greatest gifts we, as women entrepreneurs, can bestow. As we step into our own power, the significance of this role becomes apparent. We become not just businesswomen, but leaders, role models, and inspirers, all wrapped into one.

When we decide to step into our power and embrace the journey of empowerment, we become the beacon that lights the path for others. Our actions, our successes, our failures, and most importantly, our resilience, all serve as learning experiences for others. It's important to note that the act of empowerment isn't simply about sharing our success stories; it's about sharing our entire journey.

Sharing our journey is about being open and honest about our struggles and our victories. It's about admitting that there were times we were scared, unsure, or felt like giving up. It's about showing others that despite those times, we carried on. We stayed committed to our vision, we held on to our self-belief, and we persisted. It's about letting others know that they too can experience fear, doubt, and uncertainty, and still come out successful on the other side. That's true empowerment.

When we think of the power to empower others, it's not limited to those immediately around us or within our field of expertise. It can be as simple as sharing our experiences in a blog, writing a book, delivering a speech, or hosting a podcast. The important thing is to share, to reach out, and to touch the lives of others with our story.

Moreover, empowering others doesn't end with sharing our journey. It also involves creating opportunities for others to grow, learn, and thrive. This could involve creating mentorship programs, investing in women-led start-ups, hosting networking events, or leading workshops and seminars. The goal here is not just to inspire, but to provide tangible support and resources to fuel their journey.

As we rise in our power, we become custodians of our own narrative, able to shape the discourse of what it means to be a successful woman entrepreneur. By stepping into our power, we're not just succeeding as individuals, we're changing the entrepreneurial landscape for all women. Each of us, in our own unique way, is contributing to a more diverse, inclusive, and equitable business world.

Therefore, I urge you to harness your power to empower. Take pride in your journey and share it with others. Be a mentor, be a supporter, be an enabler. Let your story inspire, let your actions guide, and let your success empower. Remember, our power as women entrepreneurs isn't just measured by the businesses we build; it's also seen in the lives we touch, the changes we inspire, and the legacy we leave.

Stepping into your power isn't just about your journey, but the journeys you inspire along the way. Now, that's the true measure of entrepreneurial power!

The strength in community

As we traverse through the winding path of entrepreneurship, one truth remains steadfast and unshakeable: we're stronger together. Harnessing the power of community, gathering individuals who share common goals and aspirations, brings forth a collective strength that is often the propelling force in an entrepreneurial journey.

Communities are not just about networking; they are about nurturing relationships and fostering mutual growth. They are about shared experiences, collective wisdom, and the power of collaboration. As a female entrepreneur, I've found immense value in being a part of such a vibrant ecosystem of like-minded individuals who, much like me, are navigating the ebbs and flows of entrepreneurship.

Building a supportive community is as much about giving as it is about receiving. It's about sharing your knowledge, expertise, and experience. It's about lending a helping hand when a fellow entrepreneur stumbles and celebrating their successes as your own. It's about fostering an environment of trust, respect, and mutual support. It's about creating a space where everyone feels heard, valued, and empowered.

In building your community, be intentional about diversity. Seek individuals with varied experiences, backgrounds, and perspectives. Entrepreneurship isn't a one-size-fits-all journey, and the richness of a diverse community can provide invaluable insights and spark innovative solutions. The uniqueness of each member is what makes the community strong, resourceful, and resilient.

As you build your community, remember that it's a two-way street. Be as willing to seek help as you are to provide it. Let vulnerability and authenticity be the foundations of your relationships. Share your challenges, your fears, your triumphs, and your lessons.

Leverage technology to nurture and grow your community. With the digital world bringing people closer than ever before, we have the unique advantage of building and being a part of global communities. Use social media, digital platforms, and online forums not just to connect, but also to collaborate, learn, and grow together.

As we delve deeper into the idea of community-building, I want you to envision it not as a mere networking tool, but rather as a tapestry woven with diverse threads of mutual growth, camaraderie, and shared purpose. This tapestry, your tribe, can act as a fortress, shielding you from the solitary elements of the entrepreneurial journey, and providing a nurturing environment that bolsters confidence and encourages innovation.

Creating such a tribe requires mindful effort and conscious intention. A haphazardly constructed group will lack the depth of connection and mutual understanding required to truly flourish. Start with clear objectives in mind. What do you hope to gain from this community, and equally importantly, what do you have to offer? These questions are not designed to make you appear selfish, but rather to ensure that the community you build serves a clear purpose and fosters reciprocal relationships.

Also, bear in mind that although you may be the one spearheading the creation of your tribe, the essence of a successful community lies in collective ownership. Encourage active participation and create a sense of belonging among members. This could be through regular interactive sessions, shared decision-making, or even collaborative projects. In this process, you'll realize that every member, including yourself, is both a teacher and a student, learning from and contributing to the community's collective wisdom.

The beauty of the entrepreneurial journey lies in its unpredictability and variety. As such, your tribe should mirror this diversity. It should be a beautiful amalgamation of individuals from different walks of life, each adding their unique value and perspective to the collective. This diversity is what sets your community apart and gives it an edge, fostering innovation and out-of-the-box thinking.

Yet, amidst this diversity, it's crucial to establish a common ground – a shared vision or goal that unifies the group. This shared purpose is the glue that holds the tribe together, providing a sense of direction and maintaining cohesion even when faced with challenges or disagreements.

Additionally, while building your tribe, remain cognizant of the ever-evolving nature of communities. As your entrepreneurial journey progresses, your needs may change, and so might those of your community members. Be open to this evolution, adapting and growing with your tribe.

Moreover, bear in mind that building a community isn't a race; it's more akin to a marathon. It's a long-term commitment that requires patience, effort, and above all, genuine interest in the growth and well-being of all members.

In the grand scheme of your entrepreneurial journey, your tribe is your haven, your powerhouse, and your cheer squad, all rolled into one. It's a testament to the age-old wisdom that unity is strength. As you navigate the waters of entrepreneurship, let your tribe be your compass, guiding you towards shared success and growth. Your journey may have started as a solo endeavor, but with your tribe by your side, it need not continue that way. Together, you are invincible. Together, you rise.

Leveraging diversity

Embracing diversity is an incredibly powerful, transformative tool, particularly in the context of entrepreneurship. A diverse mindset is the fuel that propels you forward on your journey, allowing you to explore new territories and gain a more comprehensive understanding of the vast entrepreneurial landscape. In this section, we'll delve into the importance of celebrating and utilizing diverse ideas and perspectives in entrepreneurship, and the profound impact it can have on your entrepreneurial journey.

We often hear the term 'diversity' used in the context of social justice, equality, and representation, which, of course, are critical. However, in an entrepreneurial setting, diversity goes beyond these dimensions. It involves inviting a multiplicity of ideas, experiences, and perspectives into your business realm and leveraging them to create innovative solutions, increase adaptability, and drive growth.

Diversity invites us to see the world through multiple lenses, each offering its unique viewpoint and interpretation. This expanded vision not only enriches our understanding but also aids in identifying and capitalizing on new opportunities. As an entrepreneur, a diverse perspective can be the difference between remaining stuck in a rut and pivoting towards an unexplored, potentially prosperous direction.

Moreover, by consciously incorporating diversity into your entrepreneurial mindset, you are laying the groundwork for a more inclusive business culture. This inclusivity, in turn, fosters a sense of belonging among team members, partners, and even customers, thereby bolstering loyalty, satisfaction, and engagement.

But how exactly do we leverage diversity in entrepreneurship? For starters, it begins with being open and receptive to different viewpoints and experiences. When faced with a challenge or decision, seek input from a variety of sources. These could be your team members, mentors, peers from diverse industries, or even feedback from customers. You'd be surprised at the richness of ideas and solutions that can emerge from such a collective brainstorming process.

Further, recognize and celebrate the unique qualities and strengths of each member of your team or community. Encourage them to bring their full selves to the table, including their backgrounds, experiences, and insights. This inclusivity not only enriches the overall knowledge base but also fosters a sense of unity and mutual respect within the group.

In addition to welcoming diverse perspectives, it's crucial to implement them effectively. This might involve stepping out of your comfort zone and embracing unconventional methods or ideas. It may require you to adapt and evolve your existing business strategies. Remember, in the face of diversity, rigidity is a roadblock. Flexibility, on the other hand, is your passport to growth and innovation.

Finally, keep in mind that the journey to leveraging diversity is not a one-off event but rather a continuous process of learning, adapting, and growing. It requires a conscious commitment to being open, inclusive, and respectful of all perspectives.

The depth of diversity extends beyond race, ethnicity, or gender—it encompasses a spectrum of characteristics that make us unique. This includes diverse skills, experiences, cognitive styles, age, education, and even geographic locations. When you think about diversity in such broad terms, you start to realize the tremendous value it brings to the entrepreneurial table. It isn't just about fairness or representation—it's a strategic advantage.

Consider the instance of an entrepreneur who has built a team comprising members from different professional backgrounds. One is a marketing genius, another a tech whiz, the third a finance guru, and the fourth an operations specialist. Each brings a distinct perspective, a unique problem-solving approach, and a wealth of insights from their respective fields. The collective expertise of such a diverse team becomes the entrepreneur's most powerful resource, driving innovation and business growth.

Imagine another scenario where an entrepreneur seeking to expand her business globally actively seeks perspectives from individuals in different geographic locations. She learns about cultural nuances, consumer preferences, and local business practices, insights she couldn't have gleaned otherwise. This cultural diversity allows her to customize her business strategy to resonate with a global audience.

Then there's cognitive diversity, perhaps the most intriguing form of diversity. It refers to the different ways people perceive, think, and approach problems. Encouraging cognitive diversity means fostering an environment where team members feel comfortable expressing their ideas, no matter how unconventional or 'out of the box' they may seem. The result? A hotbed for innovative ideas and breakthrough solutions!

Embracing diversity is not without its challenges. It requires active listening, open-mindedness, and a willingness to step out of our comfort zones. It also requires us to challenge our biases and preconceived notions. But the rewards of embracing diversity far outweigh the challenges. A Harvard Business Review study found that diverse teams were able to solve problems faster than cognitively similar teams. Another study found that companies with more diverse management teams have 19% higher revenues due to innovation. These are compelling indicators of the power of diversity in driving entrepreneurial success.

To leverage diversity effectively, one must cultivate an inclusive mindset. This means not only inviting diverse perspectives but also ensuring they are valued and considered. It means creating a culture where every voice matters where every idea is heard, and where everyone feels they belong. It also means being willing to learn, unlearn, and relearn.

Conclusion

As we reach the end of this chapter, it's my hope that you're filled with a newfound appreciation for the power of relationships and community in entrepreneurship. Building your tribe is far more than a strategic move—it is a journey of personal growth, shared wisdom, and mutual support.

Let's recall that networking is not just about exchanging business cards or sending LinkedIn requests. It's about creating a network of meaningful relationships with like-minded people who understand your journey and can provide invaluable advice, encouragement, and insight along the way. Remember, every conversation is an opportunity to learn something new and to expand your perspective.

Our exploration of finding mentors and role models illustrated the powerful impact these figures can have on your entrepreneurial journey. They offer not only their expertise, but also their lived experiences, successes, and failures, which you can draw from as you navigate your own path.

We also delved into the strength that comes from being part of a supportive community. A community is like a sanctuary, where you're encouraged, uplifted, and inspired. It's a place where you can find a listening ear, sound advice, and even opportunities for collaboration. It truly amplifies the saying, "Together, we are stronger."

Finally, we discussed the significance of diversity within your tribe. Embracing diversity fosters innovation, as it brings together a myriad of ideas, perspectives, and experiences. It encourages you to think beyond your usual scope and allows for more inclusive and comprehensive solutions. As an entrepreneur, leveraging diversity can be a game changer.

As we conclude this chapter, I encourage you to actively begin building your tribe if you haven't started yet. Seek out mentors, join communities, start conversations, and value the diversity that each member brings. Understand that this process takes time and patience—it's not about quantity, but quality.

Building your tribe is akin to weaving a tapestry of diverse threads, each one bringing its unique strength and color to the whole. It's about creating a circle of influence that pushes you to grow, helps you stand in the face of challenges, and celebrates your victories with you. Here's to the power of the tribe, the strength of community, and the incredible journey that entrepreneurship is. The journey to success might be a steep climb, but with your tribe, you will never have to walk alone.

Questions

The following questions have been carefully designed to help you reflect on Chapter 7: Building Your Tribe. Taking the time to deeply engage with these questions will reinforce the principles and strategies discussed and help you translate them into practical steps for your unique entrepreneurial journey. Remember, there are no right or wrong answers here—these questions are meant to stimulate thought and encourage introspection.

1. How would you define your current professional network? What strengths do you see in it, and where could improvements be made?

2. Who are the people in your life or career that you consider as role models or mentors? Why? If you do not currently have a mentor, who would you ideally want to learn from?

3. In what ways has been part of a community (professional or personal) benefited your entrepreneurial journey so far?

4. What steps can you take to foster a more diverse and inclusive network? How can you consciously seek out and value diverse perspectives in your business?

5. How can you make networking more purposeful and meaningful for you? What could change in your current approach to networking?

6. How do you plan to leverage the strengths of your tribe to boost your business and personal growth?

7. What are some ways you can give back to your community or network? How can you contribute to the growth and success of others?

Remember, the value of these questions lies in the honest self-reflection and the actionable insights they can offer. As you engage with these questions, embrace openness, and strive for continual growth and learning.

Exercises

The exercises below have been designed to dovetail with the concepts and strategies shared in Chapter 7: Building Your Tribe. They are practical tasks, intended to help you implement what you've learned and reinforce your understanding of the chapter's content. By investing time in these exercises, you'll not only deepen your comprehension but also take proactive steps towards shaping your entrepreneurial journey.

Exercise 1: Map Your Network Draw a mind map of your existing professional network. Include all connections you can think of and categorize them into groups such as mentors, peers, industry influencers, etc.

Exercise 2: Reach Out Identify three individuals within your network that you've not spoken to in a while. Reach out to them and renew the connection.

Exercise 3: Identify a Potential Mentor Identify someone in your field whom you admire and would like to learn from. Develop a plan on how you can approach them for mentorship.

Exercise 4: Join a New Community Research and find a new community related to your field. This could be an online forum, a professional organization, or a local meetup group. Join the community and participate in their activities.

Exercise 5: Evaluate Diversity Examine your existing network for diversity. If you find it lacking, list actions you can take to broaden your connections to include diverse perspectives.

Exercise 6: Implement a Regular Networking Routine Plan a regular networking routine, such as attending an event once a month, or setting up a coffee meeting with a contact once a week.

Exercise 7: Give Back Find a way to give back to your network. This could be offering mentorship to a less experienced individual, volunteering in community activities, or sharing useful resources.

As you embark on these exercises, remember that building your tribe is not a one-time activity, but a continuous process. These tasks are steps towards creating a robust network that can support and elevate your entrepreneurial journey. So embrace the process and remember, every connection you make is a vital part of your tribe.

Affirmation

Affirmations are a powerful tool to help you reinforce positive beliefs, set the tone for your day, and keep you focused on your goals. They serve as reminders of your capabilities and the mindset you wish to maintain. In line with Chapter 7: Building Your Tribe, this affirmation focuses on the strength and value of your network, and your ability to foster meaningful connections.

Affirmation:

"I am a magnet for meaningful connections. I am open, approachable, and valuable to my network. I understand that each relationship contributes uniquely to my journey. I celebrate the diversity of my tribe, and I continuously strive to strengthen these bonds. Together, we thrive."

Recite this affirmation daily, preferably in the morning to start your day on a positive note. Try saying it out loud, write it on a sticky note and put it where you'll see it regularly, or simply meditate on it. Let the words sink in and resonate with your thoughts and actions throughout the day.

By regularly using this affirmation, you're setting a positive intention to not just build, but to foster and value your tribe. Remember that the community you build serves not only as a resource but also as a reflection of your journey. So, allow this affirmation to inspire you to actively and passionately engage with your tribe every day.

"Don't limit yourself. Many people limit themselves to what they think they can do. You can go as far as your mind lets you. What you believe, remember, you can achieve." - Mary Kay Ash

Chapter 8:
Stepping into Your Power.

The name itself evokes an array of emotions, doesn't it? This chapter is all about harnessing the potential within you and stepping into the spotlight as an entrepreneur who not just dreams, but also dares to achieve. It's about amplifying your unique capabilities, emboldening your ambitions, and allowing yourself to become the best version of the entrepreneur you are destined to be.

This might sound daunting, but I assure you, it's a transformation that happens gradually, one courageous action at a time. It's about tapping into that inner reservoir of strength, resilience, and creativity, to face every obstacle, seize every opportunity, and celebrate every victory. Remember, your power lies not in the absence of challenges, but in your ability to overcome them.

As we delve deeper into this chapter, let's take a moment to fully understand what 'stepping into your power' truly means. It's not about becoming someone else or taking on an entirely new persona. Instead, it's about discovering and owning who you truly are as an individual, and more importantly, as an entrepreneur. It's about acknowledging your strengths, accepting your weaknesses, and embracing all that makes you unique.

Have you ever noticed how some entrepreneurs seem to radiate a certain energy, a sense of command and assurance? That's the power we're talking about! They've learned to tap into their innate capabilities, cultivated their confidence, and are not afraid to assert their worth. And guess what? You can do it too!

Often, we find ourselves restrained by our perceived limitations. The fear of failure, the impostor syndrome, the overwhelming sense of responsibility, they all tend to put us in a box, restricting our potential. This chapter is about breaking free from that box. It's about pushing your boundaries, challenging your limits, and surprising yourself with what you're capable of achieving.

'Stepping into Your Power' is also about recognizing the fact that you can create, influence, and transform. Your entrepreneurial journey is not merely about managing a successful business; it's also about leaving an impactful legacy. It's about the footprints you leave behind, the hearts you touch, and the difference you make.

Every entrepreneur has a different journey, every journey has its unique trials, and every trial holds within it the opportunity to grow and flourish. And as we delve deeper into the many facets of 'Stepping into Your Power', I hope that you will find the inspiration and the strength to transform trials into triumphs and challenges into opportunities. It's time to let your light shine bright, for it's your time to step into your power! Let's embrace this journey together with resilience, confidence, and a fierce determination to succeed.

Celebrating milestones

Isn't it fascinating how we humans love to celebrate? Birthdays, anniversaries, national holidays, we have numerous occasions where we gather with our loved ones to rejoice and create memories. But how often do we take the time to celebrate our personal achievements, particularly in our entrepreneurial journey?

Celebrating milestones is an essential part of that journey. Each milestone you reach is a testament to your hard work, your perseverance, and your dedication. It's a tangible marker of your progress towards your vision. But, most importantly, it's a crucial reminder that you are moving forward, no matter how slow or fast the pace may be. So, let's explore why we should take a moment to pause, reflect, and revel in each one of our achievements.

Our achievements are like checkpoints in a marathon. They motivate us, rejuvenate our energy, and give us the much-needed push to continue forward. When you pause to celebrate a milestone, you're taking a moment to acknowledge your effort and the progress you've made. This recognition, in turn, fuels your self-confidence and reinforces your belief in your capabilities.

However, celebrating milestones isn't just about boosting morale. It's also an opportunity to assess and reflect on your journey so far. It's like taking a breather during a marathon to hydrate and regain strength, but also to observe the track you've covered and plan for the path ahead. This reflection allows you to reassess your strategies, learn from your experiences, and prepare for the next phase of your journey.

When we talk about celebrating milestones, it's essential to understand that it's not just about the significant breakthroughs or the 'big wins.' Small victories matter too. In fact, they are just as, if not more, important. Why? Because it's the small wins that gradually build up to the significant breakthroughs. Every step you take, every task you complete, every challenge you overcome, is bringing you one step closer to your vision.

Recognizing and celebrating these small wins fosters a positive mindset. It encourages you to appreciate your journey, instead of constantly worrying about the destination. It trains you to find joy in the process, which ultimately enhances your overall entrepreneurial experience.

As I further delve into this topic, I want to reiterate the profound impact of celebrating your milestones. Each milestone reflects your growth, a tangible symbol of your determination, and a beacon illuminating your path to success. But in the hustle and bustle of our entrepreneurial journey, we sometimes forget to recognize these important markers.

One reason we might overlook our accomplishments is because we're so focused on our goals that we forget to value the process that leads us there. We're constantly striving, pushing ourselves to do more, to achieve more. And while ambition is vital to success, it's equally important to pause, reflect and relish in the fruits of our labor.

You see, celebrating milestones isn't merely about patting ourselves on the back. It serves a broader, more meaningful purpose. It helps us to track our progress, to see how far we've come from where we started. Each milestone, no matter how small, is a piece of our entrepreneurial journey. Together, they form the unique tapestry of our experiences, challenges, lessons, and achievements.

Moreover, celebrating milestones helps to cultivate a positive mindset. It shifts our perspective from what we haven't achieved to what we have accomplished. This shift is empowering. It breeds confidence and resilience, both of which are crucial for entrepreneurial success. When we take the time to recognize our achievements, we're reinforcing our self-efficacy. We're validating our capabilities and fueling our motivation to keep pushing forward, to keep striving for success.

And let's not forget the impact of celebration on our mental well-being. The journey of an entrepreneur is often laden with stress and uncertainty. Pausing to celebrate our milestones provides a much-needed respite from this relentless pressure. It brings joy and satisfaction, lifting our spirits, and injecting a dose of positivity into our journey.

But how do we celebrate these milestones? Well, the way you choose to celebrate is entirely up to you. It could be as simple as taking a moment to acknowledge your achievement. It could be sharing your accomplishment with your team or your loved ones. Or perhaps, it could be treating yourself to something special, a small reward for your hard work.

The key is to make it meaningful for you. Because each of your milestones is a testament to your journey, to your courage, your resilience, and your unwavering commitment to your vision. So, take the time to honor them, to celebrate them, and to draw inspiration and strength from them.

Remember, the path to entrepreneurial success isn't defined by the destination alone. It's also about the journey, the process, the milestones that mark your progress. So, dear reader, as you continue your entrepreneurial journey, I encourage you to celebrate each milestone. Because each one is a step forward, a mark of progress, and a victory worth celebrating. And above all, they are reminders of your power, your potential, and your capability to turn your vision into reality. So, step into your power, and let your milestones be the shining beacons guiding your path to success.

There's a tale of a vibrant woman named Rosa. She was a woman of great dreams and aspirations, dreaming of owning her own business, one that combined her passion for healthy living and her background in nutrition. Though she held a comfortable job in a well-known company, she knew deep inside that the 9 to 5 life was not her destiny.

One day, after a series of sleepless nights filled with ideas and what-ifs, Rosa woke up with a surge of determination. She looked at herself in the mirror and said, "It's time, Rosa. It's time to step into your power."

Taking the plunge wasn't easy. Doubts, uncertainties, and fear of failure often visited Rosa, but she chose to see them as friendly reminders that she was moving out of her comfort zone and into new, uncharted territory. Every decision she made, every challenge she faced, was a testament to her resilience and determination.

Rosa started small. She began by creating a blog where she shared her knowledge about nutrition and healthy living. It was a hit. People loved her content and started asking for more. This success led her to develop a line of natural health supplements, born out of her deep research and understanding of her field.

She worked tirelessly, not just to ensure the success of her business but to make a positive impact on her community. She hired a diverse team, focused on local sourcing, and even started a foundation to promote healthy living among the underprivileged.

One day, during an interview with a local business journal, the interviewer asked Rosa how she felt about her journey. Rosa looked back at the path she had carved for herself and responded, "I am grateful for each moment, every milestone, each setback. They've shaped me and made me the entrepreneur I am today. I've learned that success isn't just about the destination, but about the journey itself."

The story of Rosa and her entrepreneurial journey inspires us all. She stepped into her power, embraced her journey with open arms, and left a positive imprint on her community. Rosa's tale is a powerful reminder that stepping into our power doesn't just change our lives; it can change the world.

Reflecting on your journey

Our journey as entrepreneurs is much like an enriching novel. Each chapter brims with its own set of ups and downs, successes and setbacks, lessons, and learnings. The past is etched with experiences that have molded us into who we are today, shaping our thoughts, decisions, and actions. And while the allure of the future can often lead us to overlook our past, there is immense value in reflecting on our journey, for it carries the wisdom of our experiences and the lessons they hold.

As we stand on the brink of each new venture, it becomes crucial to pause and look back on the journey we've traversed so far. Reflecting on our journey is not about dwelling on our past; it's about using our past as a tool for growth and learning. It's about recognizing the patterns, understanding the missteps, appreciating the triumphs, and distilling the wisdom that lies within these experiences.

The first step to meaningful reflection is honest self-assessment. It involves taking a transparent, objective look at our past actions, decisions, and their outcomes. Did we achieve what we set out to? If yes, what were the key factors that contributed to our success? If not, where did we stumble? This level of self-awareness can provide valuable insights into our strengths, weaknesses, and areas for improvement.

Reflection also helps us understand the lessons hidden in our failures and successes alike. Each misstep brings with it a valuable lesson, a nugget of wisdom that can help us navigate future challenges. By the same token, our successes hold lessons of their own. They reinforce the strategies that work, the approaches that yield results, and the mindset that fosters success.

But reflection isn't just about dissecting the past; it's also about looking forward. It's about applying the insights and learnings from our journey to our future endeavors. It's about taking our newfound wisdom and using it as a guide, a roadmap, to chart a more informed, conscious, and mindful path forward.

When we reflect on our journey and apply our learnings, we're not just better prepared to face future challenges; we're also more likely to seize opportunities. We become more adept at making informed decisions, at anticipating and mitigating risks, and at leading with resilience and confidence. We step into our power, equipped with the wisdom of our past and the promise of our future.

In life's grand tapestry, there's a delicate art to introspection and reflection. And as entrepreneurs, this art takes on a new level of importance, shaping the choices we make and the future we craft. Understanding this allows us to fine-tune our perspective, providing us a sharper lens through which we can perceive our journey, absorb its lessons, and evolve as individuals and leaders.

Understanding our journey in depth is akin to peeling back the layers of an onion. Each layer represents a unique phase, a different challenge, a distinct triumph, or a moment of realization. As we peel back each layer, we uncover the experiences that have influenced us, the decisions that have shaped us, and the lessons that have guided us.

One might wonder, 'Is it necessary to delve so deeply into the past?' The answer lies in the fact that it is not about dwelling on what was, but acknowledging how those experiences have shaped what is and what could be. Every triumph, every setback, each success, and every failure - they all come together to shape us, guiding us on our unique entrepreneurial path. Reflection is the key that unlocks these hidden treasures, bringing them to the fore, empowering us to utilize them in our journey forward.

Drawing wisdom from past experiences paves the way for mindful action. When we reflect on our journey, we don't just unravel the past; we also illuminate our path ahead. We gain a clearer understanding of our own potential and the strategies that have proven effective. We discern the practices that didn't serve us well and acknowledge the areas where we need to adapt or improve. This process helps us craft a more informed, calculated strategy for our future endeavors.

Moreover, reflecting on our journey and applying our learnings also enhances our emotional intelligence. It fosters empathy, patience, and resilience, qualities indispensable to any entrepreneur. It enables us to relate better with our team, our customers, and ourselves. It allows us to manage stress and handle challenges with greater composure, enhancing our overall mental wellbeing.

But remember, reflection is a process, not a one-time event. It's a habit that needs to be cultivated and nurtured over time. It requires patience, honesty, and an open mind. It's about creating a space where we can be alone with our thoughts, where we can listen to our inner voice, where we can truly connect with ourselves.

So dear reader, as you continue to traverse your entrepreneurial journey, I encourage you to take moments of pause, moments of reflection. Allow yourself the grace of looking back at your path, not with regret or self-criticism, but with appreciation and wisdom. Seek the lessons that lie hidden within your experiences and use them as the guiding light for your journey ahead.

Remember, the power to shape your future lies within you, etched within the contours of your journey. By reflecting on your past and applying its lessons, you're not just moving forward; you're stepping into your power. You're evolving into a more resilient, more insightful, and more empowered entrepreneur, ready to shape your destiny and leave a legacy of success.

Planning for the future

There's a certain thrill and trepidation that comes with looking into the future. The horizon that stretches out in front of us, filled with unknowns and yet, ripe with endless possibilities. The act of envisioning our personal and business growth is not just exciting but crucial as it provides the fuel to propel us forward on our entrepreneurial journey.

I often think of it as dreaming with purpose. It's not just about daydreaming or wishful thinking, it's about intentionally shaping the vision of what we want our business and personal life to look like in the future. The beauty of it is that there are no restrictions, no limitations. It's your vision; you get to choose what it looks like.

But envisioning the future isn't just about grand plans and lofty goals. It's about imagining the journey, contemplating the steps you'll need to take, and the growth you'll need to undergo to bring your vision to fruition. It involves a deep understanding of your current situation and a realistic assessment of what it will take to get where you want to go.

Envisioning your business growth involves asking yourself questions like, 'What do I want my business to look like in five years?', 'What sort of impact do I want to make?',

'Who do I want to serve?', 'What kind of team do I want to build?' or 'What do I want to be known for in my industry?'. It's about daring to dream big, but also being prepared to do what it takes to make those dreams a reality.

In parallel, envisioning personal growth is an equally important aspect. As entrepreneurs, we tend to intertwine our personal identities with our businesses. While this can create a strong sense of purpose and drive, it's essential that we also nurture our growth independent of our business.

Personal growth might involve learning new skills, investing in personal development, strengthening relationships, improving health and wellbeing, or dedicating time to passions outside of work. It's about becoming a more rounded individual who can bring a wealth of life experiences, perspectives, and resilience to the entrepreneurial journey.

Planning for the future, both business and personal, can be exciting, daunting, and downright overwhelming at times. But remember, this vision is not set in stone. It is a living, breathing entity that can adapt and grow with you. It serves as a guiding light, providing direction when you're unsure of the next step.

So, dare to dream. Dare to imagine what could be. Allow yourself the freedom to envision a future where your business thrives, and you grow, not just as an entrepreneur but as a person. This vision, this daring, is not just a dream.

It's the foundation upon which you'll build your future success.

As we delve deeper into envisioning our future and crafting our personal and business growth paths, it's important to remember that this journey is a marathon, not a sprint. I've learned that pacing our selves, practicing patience and perseverance, and celebrating small wins are critical components of sustainable success.

It's easy to get caught up in the grand vision of the future, to want to reach the destination as quickly as possible. But I've come to understand that true growth is found not just in the destination, but in the journey itself. The lessons we learn, the challenges we overcome, the resilience we build, and the people we meet along the way – these are what truly shape us as entrepreneurs and as individuals.

When planning for your future, be prepared for detours and unexpected turns. I've had my fair share of these, and while they were daunting at the time, they ultimately led me to new opportunities and experiences I wouldn't have had otherwise. They taught me to be adaptable and flexible, to be open to new possibilities, even when they veer off the path I had originally set. This adaptability is a key trait of successful entrepreneurs, and it's one that will serve you well in your journey.

In envisioning your future, I also encourage you to infuse your vision with your values and passions. As entrepreneurs, we are in a unique position to create businesses that not only generate profit, but also bring about positive change and reflect who we are as individuals. When our work aligns with our values and passions, it doesn't feel like work. Instead, it becomes an expression of our purpose and a way to make a meaningful impact.

Remember too, that your entrepreneurial journey is not one you must travel alone. Surrounding yourself with a supportive community, seeking out mentors, and forging partnerships can greatly enrich your journey and your growth. There is immense power in collaboration and in learning from those who have trodden the path before us.

As we step into the future, we also step into the unknown. This can be intimidating, but it's also where the magic happens. It's where we are pushed out of our comfort zones, where we discover new strengths, and where we find new opportunities to grow and excel.

So, let's welcome the unknown, let's embrace the journey, and let's step boldly into our future. Let's remember that we are not just entrepreneurs, but pioneers charting our own paths. And with each step we take, with each milestone we reach, we are not just building our businesses, we are also building ourselves.

Remember, the future is not a destination, but a continuous journey of growth, learning, and transformation. And as you step into your power and step into your future, I have no doubt that you will shape it into something truly extraordinary. So, dream big, plan strategically, and step confidently into the future that you are creating. The future is yours to shape, and I can't wait to see what you will make of it.

Conclusion

As we reach the closing pages of this chapter, I want to remind you that stepping into your power is more than just an action, it's a state of mind. It's a mindset that embraces every accomplishment, every setback, every lesson learned, and every milestone reached. It's a mindset that takes all these elements, both the challenges and the triumphs, and uses them as fuel to keep moving forward, to keep reaching for the stars.

The journey of entrepreneurship is not a smooth path. It is a journey that will test your resilience, your determination, your courage, and your grit. It's a journey that will require you to tap into your deepest wells of strength, to rise in the face of adversity, and to keep going even when the road gets tough.

But remember this: You are capable. You are powerful. You have everything you need within you to navigate this journey successfully. All you must do is believe in yourself, act, and step into your power. Your power lies in your unique skills, your passion, your determination, and most importantly, your mindset. This is what sets you apart. This is what makes you an entrepreneur.

As we conclude this chapter, I want to leave you with this thought: Every step you take in your entrepreneurial journey, every decision you make, every challenge you overcome is a testament to your power. And as you continue this journey, remember to celebrate each moment, each milestone, because they are all a part of your unique entrepreneurial story.

Keep learning, keep growing, keep stepping into your power. Embrace the journey and know that you are not alone. There is an entire tribe of women entrepreneurs who are rooting for you, who are on similar journeys, who are stepping into their power just like you.

Let's celebrate our power as women entrepreneurs. Let's lift each other up, support each other, learn from each other, and grow together. Because together, we are stronger. Together, we can change the world. So, let's step into our power, let's step into our future, and let's make our mark as women entrepreneurs.

This is not the end, rather it's the beginning of your new journey, stepping into your power, and I can't wait to see where this journey takes you. You are more than ready, and I am here, cheering you on every step of the way. So, go ahead, step into your power. The world is waiting to see what you'll do next. And I know it's going to be something incredible.

Keep learning, keep growing, keep stepping into your power. Embrace the journey and know that you are not alone. There is an entire tribe of women entrepreneurs who are rooting for you, who are on similar journeys, who are stepping into their power just like you.

Let's celebrate our power as women entrepreneurs. Let's lift each other up, support each other, learn from each other, and grow together. Because together, we are stronger. Together, we can change the world. So, let's step into our power, let's step into our future, and let's make our mark as women entrepreneurs.

This is not the end, rather it's the beginning of your new journey, stepping into your power, and I can't wait to see where this journey takes you. You are more than ready, and I am here, cheering you on every step of the way. So, go ahead, step into your power. The world is waiting to see what you'll do next. And I know it's going to be something incredible.

Questions

Before we delve into these questions, let's take a moment to reflect on the importance of introspection on your journey. As we explored in Chapter 8, embracing your power and taking control of your destiny is a cornerstone of entrepreneurial success. These questions will guide you in reflecting on your journey and understanding how you can step more fully into your own power. They serve as a tool to gain insights and develop strategies for your personal and professional growth. I strongly encourage you to take time to thoughtfully answer each question, and remember, there's no right or wrong answer, only your unique path.

1. How do you define your power as an entrepreneur?
2. What milestones in your entrepreneurial journey are you most proud of and why?
3. How do you reflect on your journey so far? Do you celebrate your successes and learn from your failures?
4. What steps have you taken or plan to take to empower others through your success?
5. How has your entrepreneurial journey impacted your personal growth?
6. What future plans have you envisioned for your business and personal life?

7. If you were to write a letter to your future self five years from now, what advice or encouragement would you give regarding stepping into your power?

Remember, these questions are not a test, but a reflective tool to gain deeper insights into your journey. They are meant to encourage thoughtfulness and introspection, leading to a clearer understanding of your path as an entrepreneur. Reflect on them, learn from them, and allow them to guide your journey towards stepping more fully into your power.

Exercises

I'm glad to see you are ready to embark on some exercises that will empower you to step into your power more fully. This hands-on approach is one of the most effective ways to internalize the lessons from Chapter 8 and put them into practice. Remember, these exercises are meant to be done at your own pace and revisited as often as necessary. Let's begin!

1. **Power Definition:** Write a paragraph defining what power means to you in the context of your entrepreneurial journey. Revisit and revise this definition periodically as your journey unfolds.

2. **Milestone Visualization:** Create a timeline of your entrepreneurial journey so far. Highlight the milestones you're most proud of and next to each, write a brief description of why it was significant.

3. **Reflection Journaling:** Begin a daily reflection journal. At the end of each day, write about your successes, challenges, and lessons learned. This will serve as a reminder of how far you've come and the wisdom you've gained.

4. **Empowerment Action Plan:** Develop a plan for how you can use your success to empower others. This could include mentorship, starting a foundation, or any other means that align with your vision and values.

5. **Personal Growth Mapping:** Write down the ways in which your entrepreneurial journey has contributed to your personal growth. Consider areas like confidence, resilience, leadership skills, and self-awareness.

6. **Visioning Exercise:** Create a vision board for your business and personal life for the next five years. Use images, quotes, and symbols that represent your aspirations.

7. **Letter to Your Future Self:** Write a letter to your future self five years from now. In the letter, include your hopes, fears, advice, and encouragement.

I encourage you to take these exercises seriously. They are not just activities to be completed and forgotten, but ongoing practices that can guide you as you step into your power. Remember, the journey of entrepreneurship is not a sprint, but a marathon. Every step you take in self-reflection and self-growth brings you closer to embodying your power as an entrepreneur. Enjoy the journey!

Affirmation

I'm thrilled to introduce you to an affirmation practice related to Chapter 8: Stepping into Your Power. An affirmation is a positive, empowering statement that you say to yourself, affirming your capabilities and worth. Repeating this affirmation regularly can help instill a strong sense of self-belief and confidence, reinforcing the concept of stepping into your power.

Here is your affirmation for this chapter:

"I embrace my journey with confidence and courage. I celebrate every milestone, learn from every challenge, and use my success to empower others. I am stepping into my power as an entrepreneur, shaping the future with my vision and strength."

To make the most of this affirmation, I encourage you to say it out loud to yourself each morning. Look into a mirror as you do so, and really connect with the words. Feel the truth of them in your heart and let that energy carry you throughout your day. Remember, as you step into your power, you are not just transforming your own life, but also contributing positively to the world around you. Now, go forth and embrace your power!

Conclusion

As we draw this enlightening journey to a close, I want you to imagine we're seated together in a cozy corner of a bustling café. The aroma of freshly brewed coffee wafts through the air, mixing with the scent of sweet pastries. We've been in this quiet bubble for hours now, exchanging stories, insights, and anecdotes. From conceptualizing your entrepreneurial idea to stepping into your power, we've traversed through it all. Now, it's time for us to look back on the path we've journeyed and forward to where you're going to tread.

"Unleashing Your Inner Power: The Woman Entrepreneur's Guide to Success" was written with a singular aim - to inspire, motivate, and empower you, my dear reader, on your entrepreneurial journey. We began with understanding the landscape of entrepreneurship for women, grappling with its unique challenges and opportunities. We navigated through the art of ideation and strategy building, emphasizing the essence of crafting a robust and sustainable business model.

In subsequent chapters, we established the importance of work-life harmony, a delicate balance that keeps you sane and productive amid the whirlwind of entrepreneurship. We also explored the value of building your tribe - a supportive network that aids your growth, provides insight, and acts as a comforting shoulder in times of need.

Finally, we arrived at the most invigorating part - stepping into your power. We celebrated the value of each milestone, reflected on our journey, and charted the path ahead. It was about understanding your strength and wielding it to uplift and inspire others on their entrepreneurial journey.

But remember, this is not the end, it's just the beginning. The pages of this book have offered you a road map, a guiding light. But the journey itself, with all its detours, stopovers, and final destinations, that's up to you. In your hands, you hold the power to write a success story that is uniquely yours.

You've equipped yourself with knowledge, resilience, and determination, but remember, entrepreneurship is a continuous process of learning, unlearning, and relearning. Embrace the uncertainties that lie ahead with open arms and a robust spirit.

Remember, you're not just an entrepreneur. You're a woman entrepreneur, possessing the strength, the will, the courage to create, to innovate, to inspire. You are a beacon of change, ready to make a difference, ready to unleash your power and conquer the world. You're not just building a business; you're creating a legacy.

I'd like to imagine that as we part ways, you step out of the café, the book clasped tightly in your hand, a newfound determination in your eyes, ready to embark on the journey of a lifetime. I see a sparkle in your eyes and a power radiating from you that tells me you are ready. You are ready to unleash your inner power and make your entrepreneurial dreams come true.

Thank you for letting me be a part of your journey, and I wish you all the success in the world. You've got this, and I can't wait to see where your journey takes you. Unleash your power, embrace your journey, and soar high.

Debra L. Caissie

Manufactured by Amazon.ca
Acheson, AB